PLANT LADY
EMBROIDERY

Inspiring | Educating | Creating | Entertaining

Brimming with creative inspiration, how-to projects, and useful information to enrich your everyday life, Quarto Knows is a favorite destination for those pursuing their interests and passions. Visit our site and dig deeper with our books into your area of interest. Quarto Creates, Quarto Cooks, Quarto Homes, Quarto Lives, Quarto Drives, Quarto Explores, Quarto Gifts, or Quarto Kids.

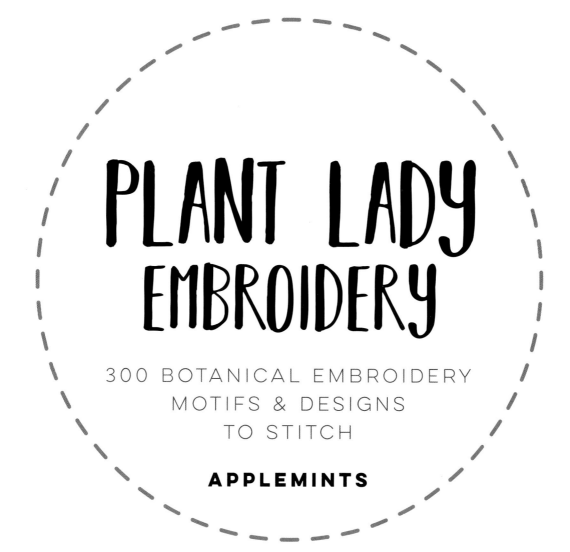

PLANT LADY
EMBROIDERY

300 BOTANICAL EMBROIDERY
MOTIFS & DESIGNS
TO STITCH

APPLEMINTS

QUARRY

Contents

Roses

Instructions: Pages 56–59
Design & Embroidery: Shigeko Kawakami

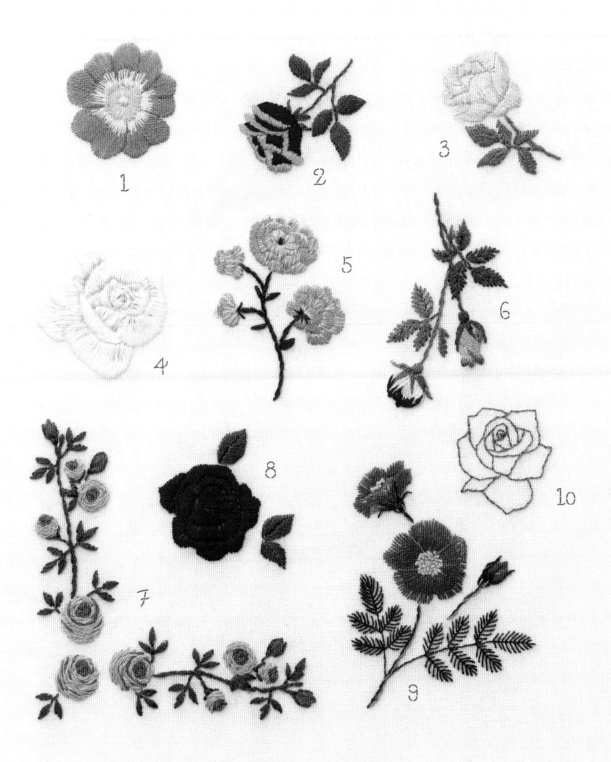

Orchids & Chrysanthemums

Instructions: Pages 60–63
Design & Embroidery: Tomiko Nakayama

21
Darwin's Orchid

22
Cycnoches

23
Dendrobium

24
Cattleya

25
Phalaenopsis
Aphrodite

26
Dancing Lady Orchid

27
Lady's Slipper

28
Masdevallia

29
Pansy Orchid

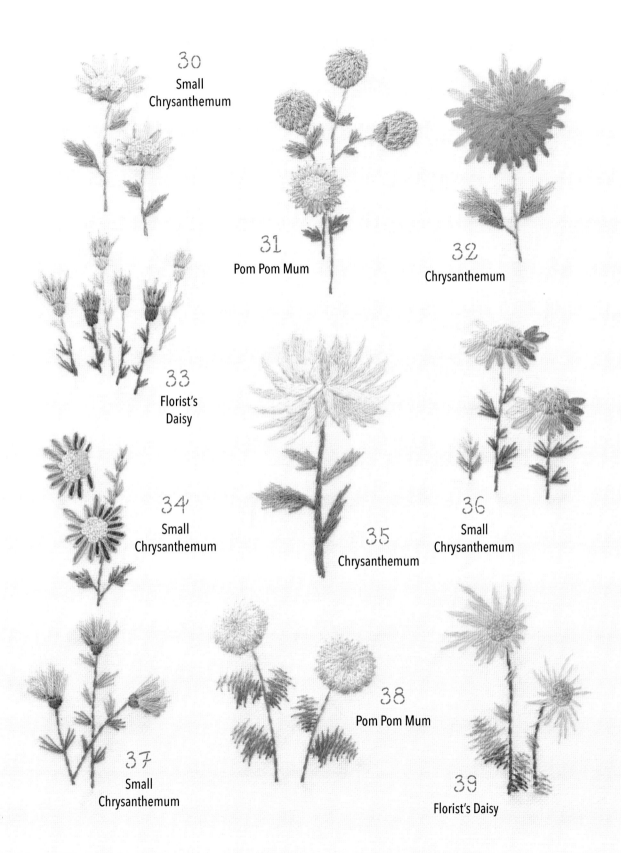

30
Small
Chrysanthemum

31
Pom Pom Mum

32
Chrysanthemum

33
Florist's
Daisy

34
Small
Chrysanthemum

35
Chrysanthemum

36
Small
Chrysanthemum

37
Small
Chrysanthemum

38
Pom Pom Mum

39
Florist's Daisy

Spring Flowers

Instructions: Pages 64–67
Design & Embroidery: Kazue Sakurai

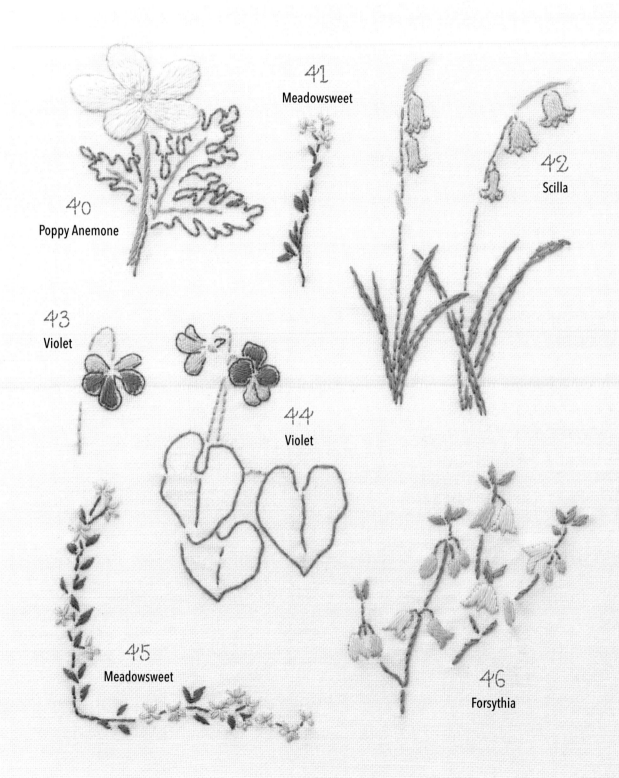

40
Poppy Anemone

41
Meadowsweet

42
Scilla

43
Violet

44
Violet

45
Meadowsweet

46
Forsythia

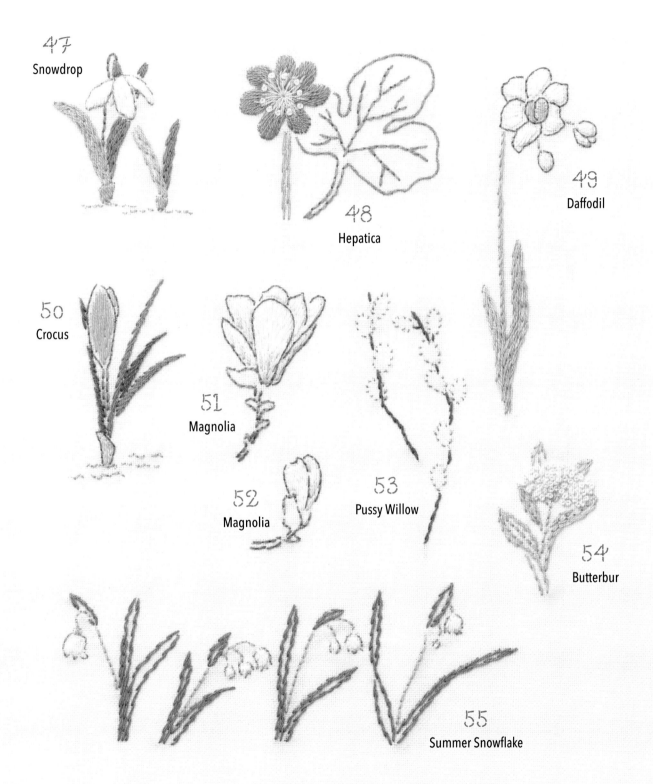

47
Snowdrop

48
Hepatica

49
Daffodil

50
Crocus

51
Magnolia

52
Magnolia

53
Pussy Willow

54
Butterbur

55
Summer Snowflake

Spring Flowers

Instructions: Pages 68–71
Design & Embroidery: Kazue Sakurai

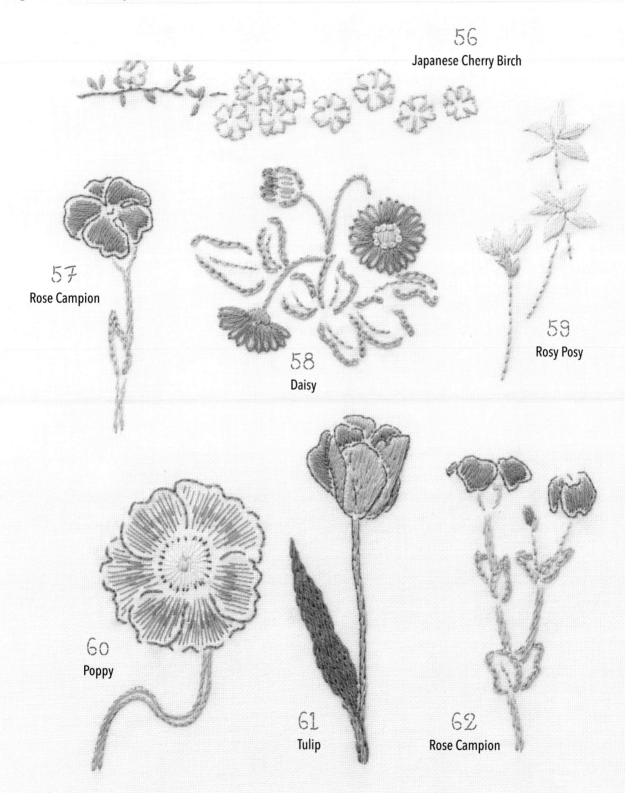

56
Japanese Cherry Birch

57
Rose Campion

58
Daisy

59
Rosy Posy

60
Poppy

61
Tulip

62
Rose Campion

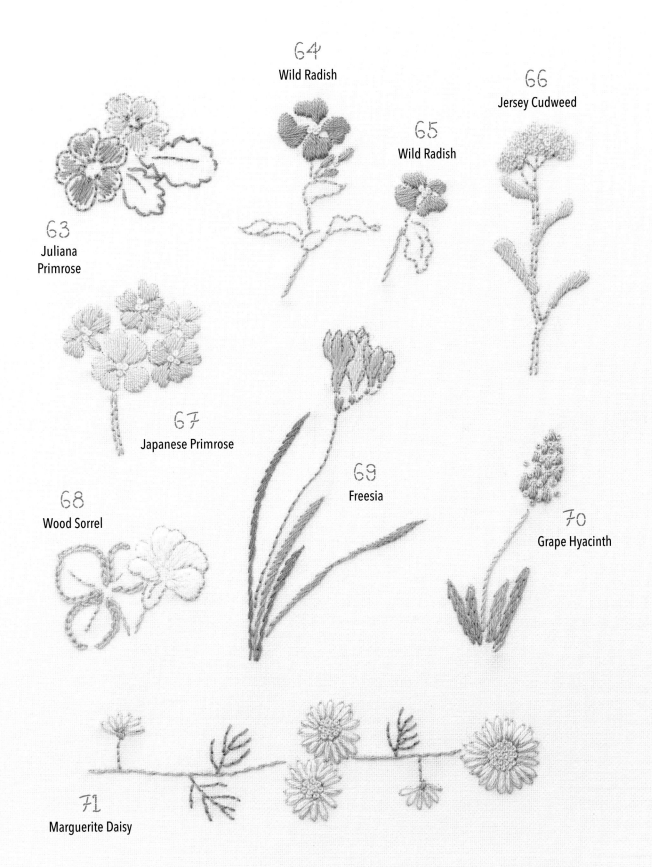

64
Wild Radish

66
Jersey Cudweed

65
Wild Radish

63
Juliana
Primrose

67
Japanese Primrose

69
Freesia

68
Wood Sorrel

70
Grape Hyacinth

71
Marguerite Daisy

Summer Flowers

Instructions: Pages 72–75
Design & Embroidery: Fumiko Saito (siesta)

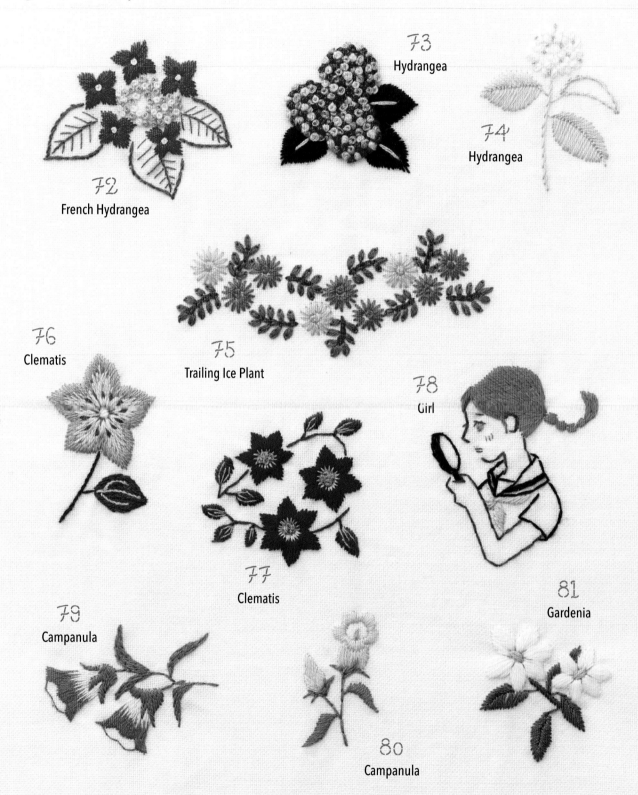

73
Hydrangea

74
Hydrangea

72
French Hydrangea

76
Clematis

75
Trailing Ice Plant

78
Girl

77
Clematis

81
Gardenia

79
Campanula

80
Campanula

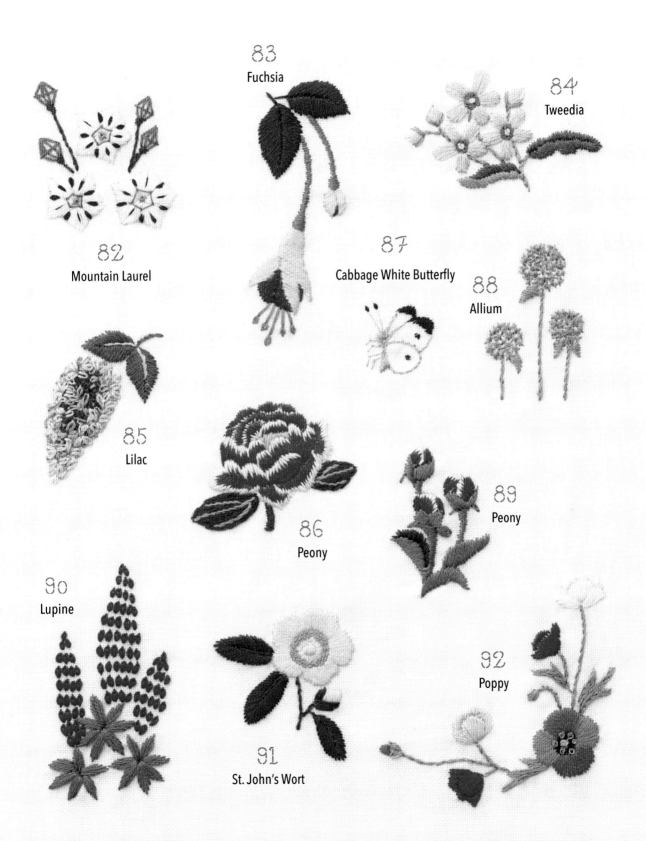

83
Fuchsia

84
Tweedia

82
Mountain Laurel

87
Cabbage White Butterfly

88
Allium

85
Lilac

86
Peony

89
Peony

90
Lupine

92
Poppy

91
St. John's Wort

Summer Flowers

Instructions: Pages 76–79
Design & Embroidery: Fumiko Saito (siesta)

94
Morning Glory

93
Sunflower

95
Sunflower

96
Girl

97
Hibiscus

98
Aster

99
Aster

100
Trumpet Vine

101
Tiger Lily

102
Edelweiss

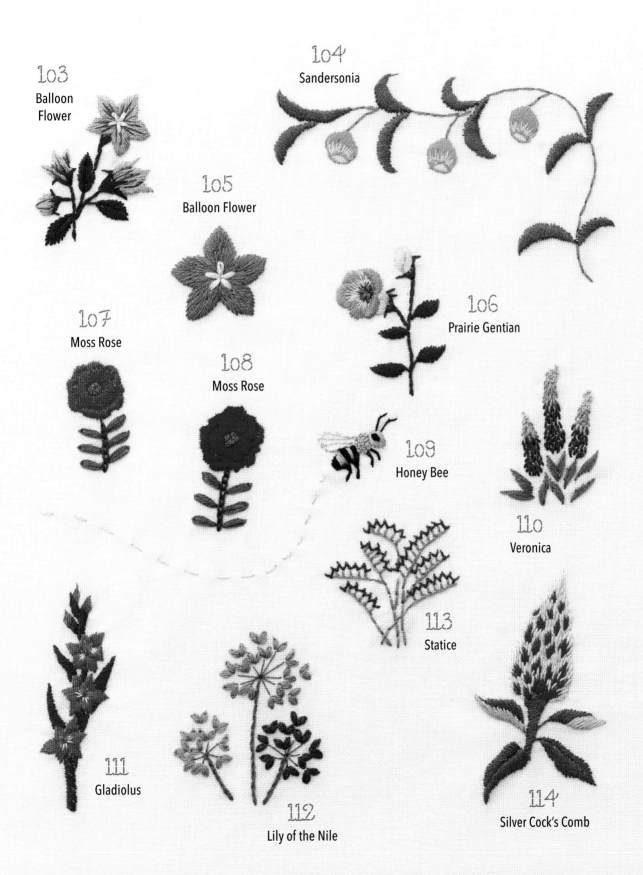

103
Balloon
Flower

104
Sandersonia

105
Balloon Flower

106
Prairie Gentian

107
Moss Rose

108
Moss Rose

109
Honey Bee

110
Veronica

111
Gladiolus

112
Lily of the Nile

113
Statice

114
Silver Cock's Comb

Autumn & Winter Flowers

Instructions: Pages 80–83
Design & Embroidery: Tomoko Watanabe

115
Chocolate Cosmos

116
Sweet Osmanthus

117
Poppy Anemone

118
Dahlia

119
Red Spider Lily

120
Pansy

121
Gentian

122
Cosmos

123
Lily

124
Sweet Osmanthus

125
Poinsettia

126
Cineraria

128
Dahlia

127
Flannel Flower

129
Hellebore

130
Kalanchoe

131
Cyclamen

133
Violet

132
Gerber Daisy

134
Violet

Flower Branches

Instructions: Pages 84–87
Design & Embroidery: Kawako Nariko

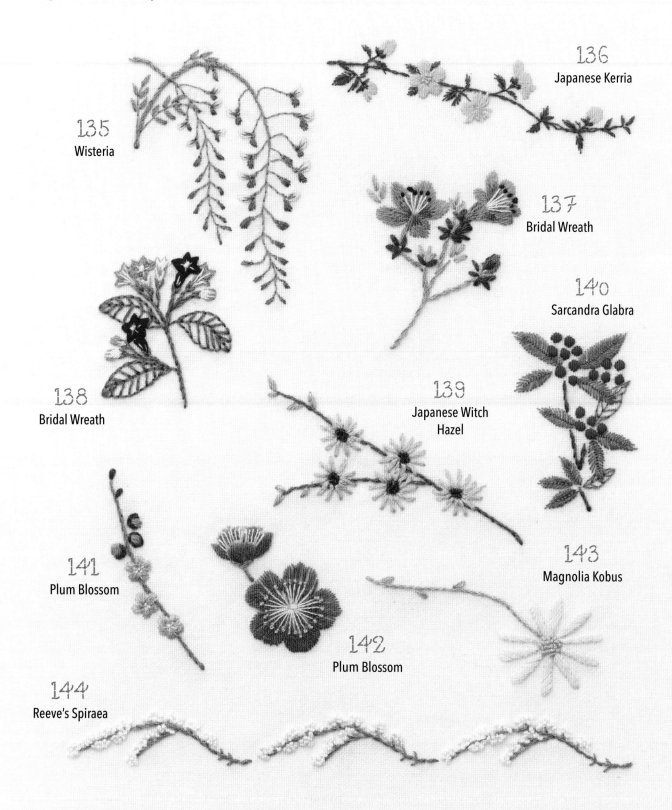

135
Wisteria

136
Japanese Kerria

137
Bridal Wreath

138
Bridal Wreath

139
Japanese Witch Hazel

140
Sarcandra Glabra

141
Plum Blossom

142
Plum Blossom

143
Magnolia Kobus

144
Reeve's Spiraea

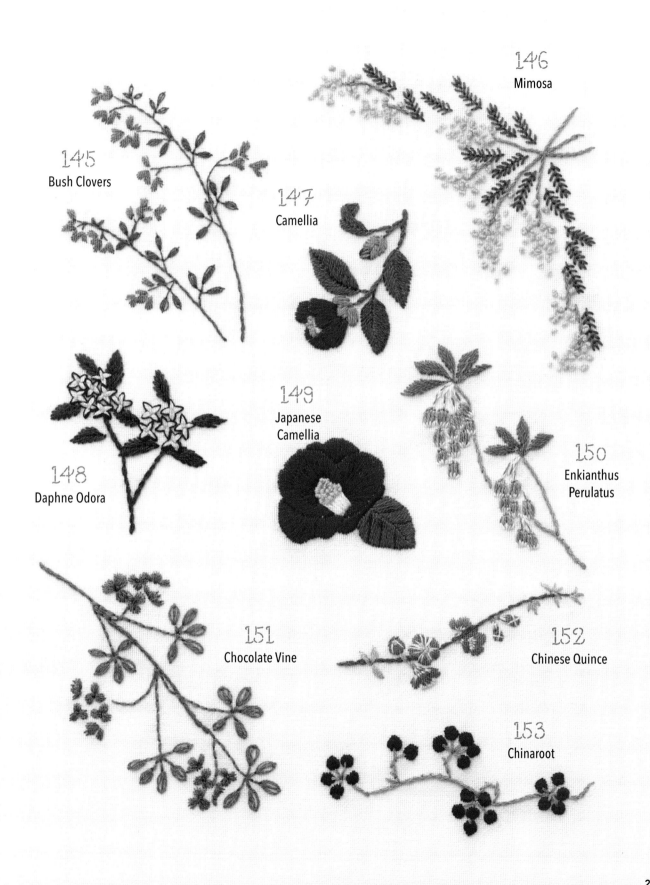

145
Bush Clovers

146
Mimosa

147
Camellia

148
Daphne Odora

149
Japanese
Camellia

150
Enkianthus
Perulatus

151
Chocolate Vine

152
Chinese Quince

153
Chinaroot

Fruit Trees

Instructions: Pages 88–91
Design & Embroidery: mogu

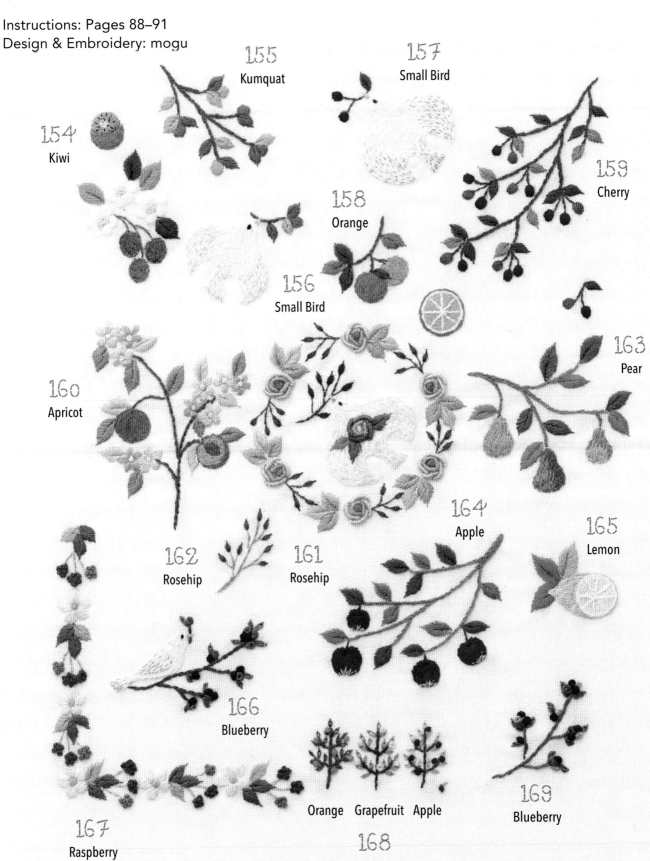

155 Kumquat

157 Small Bird

154 Kiwi

159 Cherry

158 Orange

156 Small Bird

163 Pear

160 Apricot

162 Rosehip

161 Rosehip

164 Apple

165 Lemon

166 Blueberry

Orange   Grapefruit   Apple

168

169 Blueberry

167 Raspberry

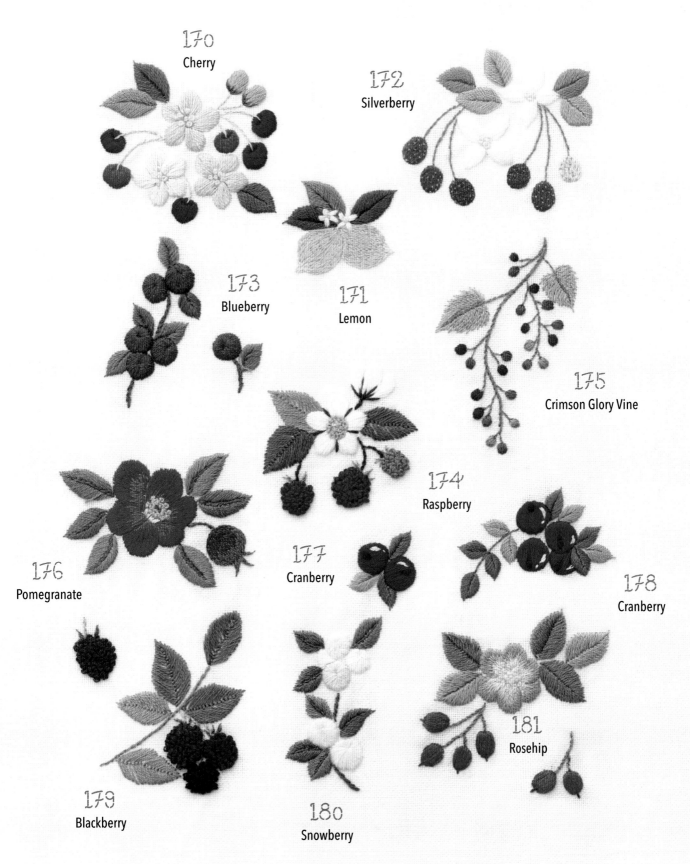

170
Cherry

172
Silverberry

173
Blueberry

171
Lemon

175
Crimson Glory Vine

174
Raspberry

176
Pomegranate

177
Cranberry

178
Cranberry

179
Blackberry

180
Snowberry

181
Rosehip

Herbs

Instructions: Pages 92–95
Design & Embroidery: Yasuko Shibata

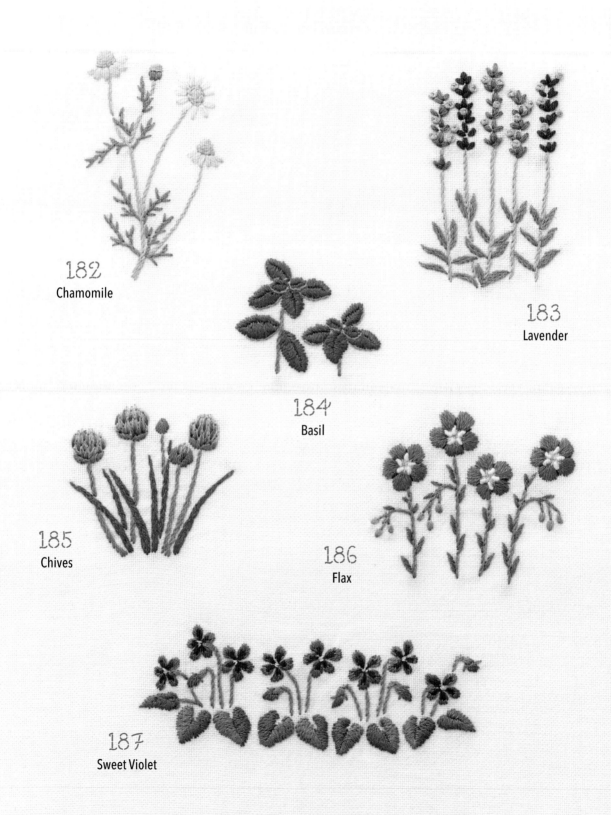

182
Chamomile

183
Lavender

184
Basil

185
Chives

186
Flax

187
Sweet Violet

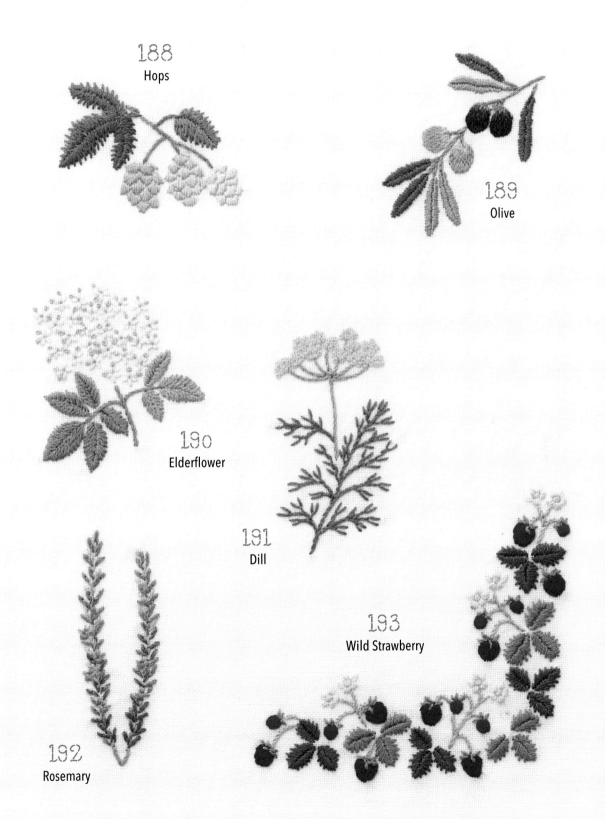

188
Hops

189
Olive

190
Elderflower

191
Dill

193
Wild Strawberry

192
Rosemary

Wildflowers & Mushrooms

Instructions: Pages 96–99
Design & Embroidery: Yasuko Sebata

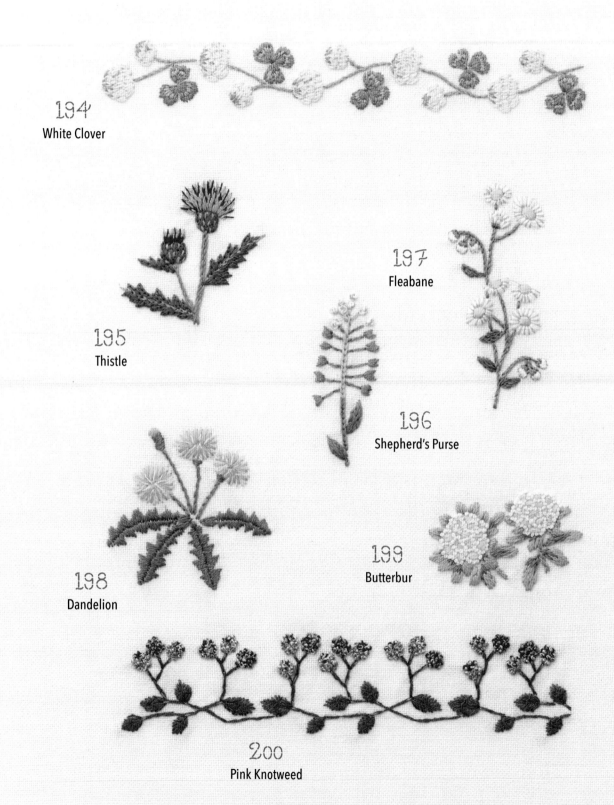

194
White Clover

195
Thistle

197
Fleabane

196
Shepherd's Purse

198
Dandelion

199
Butterbur

200
Pink Knotweed

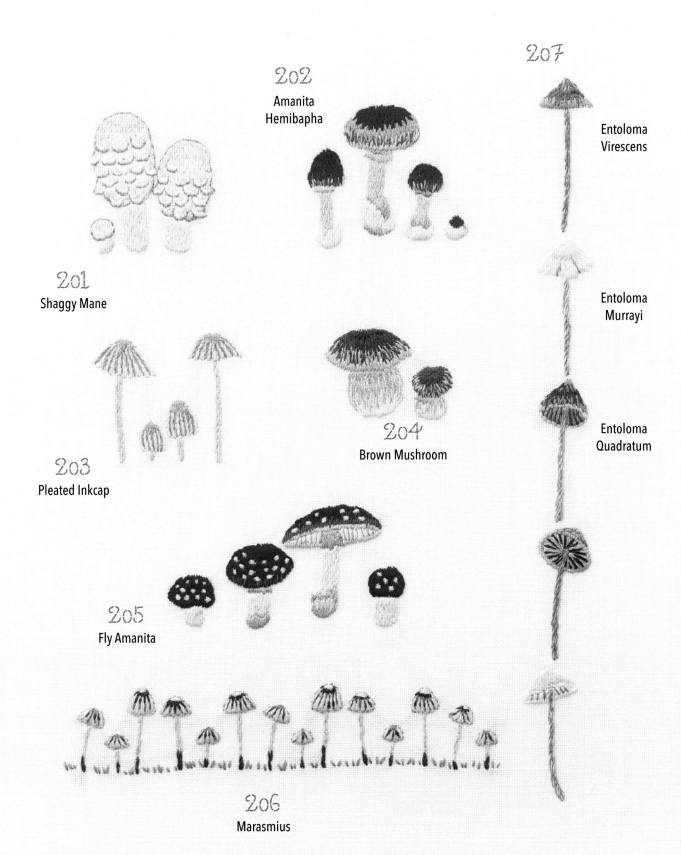

202
Amanita
Hemibapha

207

Entoloma
Virescens

201
Shaggy Mane

203
Pleated Inkcap

204
Brown Mushroom

Entoloma
Murrayi

Entoloma
Quadratum

205
Fly Amanita

206
Marasmius

Cacti & Succulents

Instructions: Pages 100–103
Design & Embroidery: Pocorute Pocochiru

208 Silver Ball Cactus

209 Dead Man's Fingers Cactus

210 Pingpong Ball Cactus

211 Gold Lace Cactus

212 Golden Barrel Cactus

Button Cactus

213 Lemon Ball Cactus

214 Arizona Rainbow Cactus

215 Spider Cactus Flower

216 Bunny Ears Cactus

Blue Barrel Cactus

217 Rose Pincushion Cactus

218
Sedum Hernandezii

219
Crassula

220
Crassula

221
San Pedro Cactus

222
Sempervivum

223
Zebra Haworthia

224
Sempervivum

225
Laulindsa

226
Candelabra Aloe

227
String of Pearls

228
Sweetheart Hoya

229
Bear's Paw

Tropical Plants

Instructions: Pages 104–107
Design & Embroidery: Sayuri Horiuchi

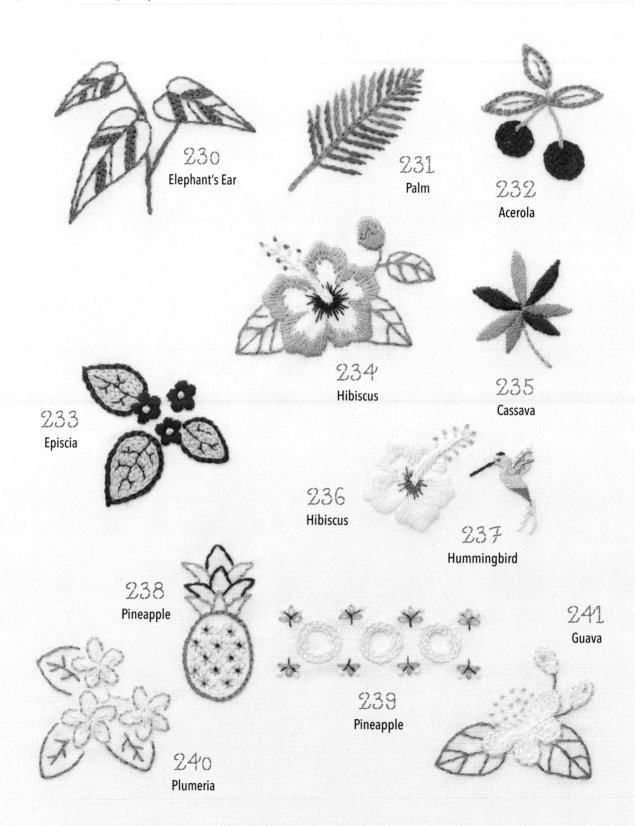

230
Elephant's Ear

231
Palm

232
Acerola

234
Hibiscus

235
Cassava

233
Episcia

236
Hibiscus

237
Hummingbird

238
Pineapple

239
Pineapple

240
Plumeria

241
Guava

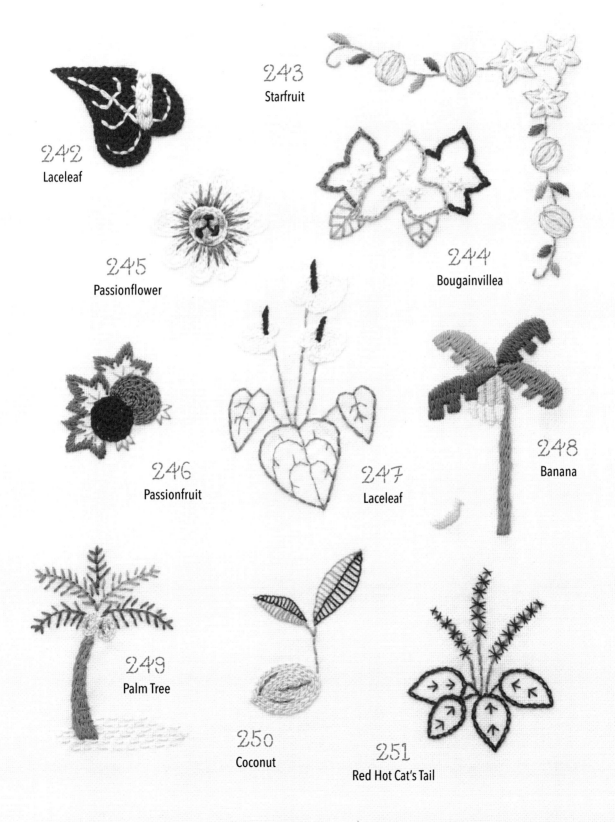

242
Laceleaf

243
Starfruit

244
Bougainvillea

245
Passionflower

246
Passionfruit

247
Laceleaf

248
Banana

249
Palm Tree

250
Coconut

251
Red Hot Cat's Tail

Foliage Plants

Instructions: Pages 108–111
Design & Embroidery: Horiuchi Sayuri

255
Japanese Laurel

252
Monstera

253
Ivy

256
Sacred Fig

257
Dischidia

254
Spider Plant

259
Sword Fern

258
Bird of Paradise

261
Alocasia Odora

260
Dracaena Cocinna

262
Dracaena Fragrans

263
Ivy

green

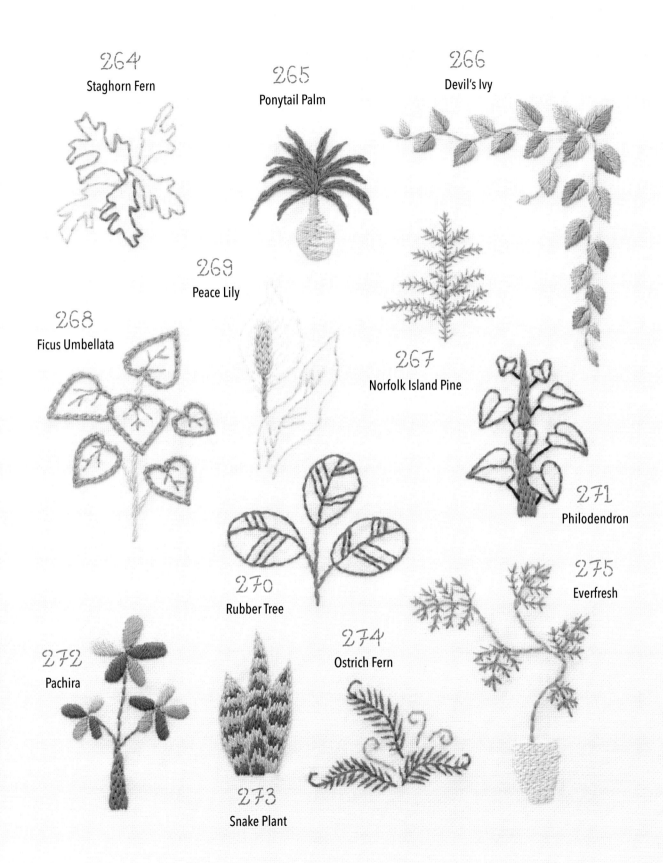

264
Staghorn Fern

265
Ponytail Palm

266
Devil's Ivy

269
Peace Lily

268
Ficus Umbellata

267
Norfolk Island Pine

271
Philodendron

270
Rubber Tree

275
Everfresh

272
Pachira

274
Ostrich Fern

273
Snake Plant

Aquatic Plants

Instructions: Pages 112–115
Design & Embroidery: Yumiko Iwata "Hanaotosya"

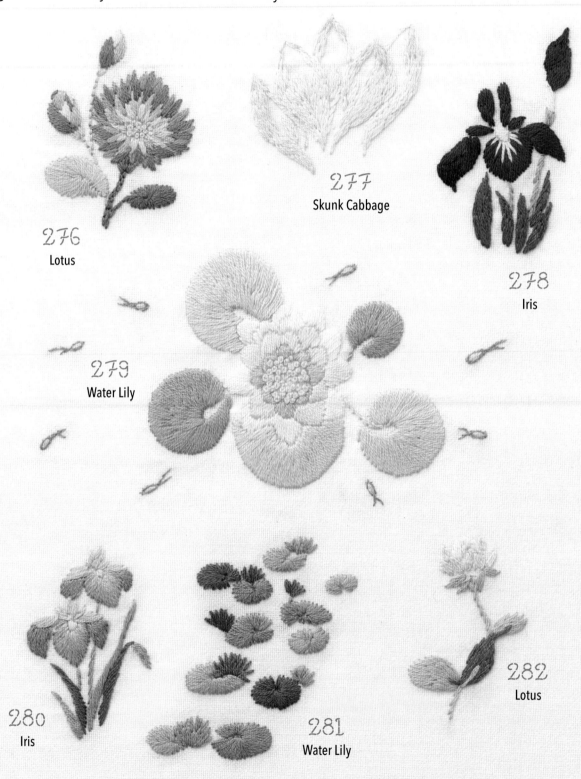

276
Lotus

277
Skunk Cabbage

278
Iris

279
Water Lily

280
Iris

281
Water Lily

282
Lotus

Water Garden

283

Willow / Hydrangea / Water Lily / Calla Lily

English Garden

Instructions: Pages 116–119
Design & Embroidery: Yumiko Iwata "Hanaotosya"

285
Roses and Rosehips

286
Roses and Rosehips

287
Geraniums

284
Roses and Fir Trees

289
Bucket

288
Trowel

290
Watering Can

291
Lamp

292
Bulb Planter

293
Hydrangeas

294
Basket

295
House

296
Roses and Poppies

298
Clematis

297
Anemone

299
Chive / Daisy / Wild Strawberry

300
Hollyhocks / Allium /
Grape Hyacinth /
Primrose /
Alyssum / Hosta

Project Inspiration Gallery

Try embroidering a pretty flower or some gorgeous greenery onto everyday items for a special touch. These colorful blooms are sure to brighten your day!

Tea Pot Cozy A cute little cactus adds some personality to a store-bought tea pot cozy.

Motif 211 on page 100

Placemat A refreshing foliage design adds color and cheer to a simple linen placemat.

Motif 272 on page 110

Brooches Stitch an elegant rose motif onto felt, then attach a pin to the back to create a wearable work of art.

Motifs 3 and 8 on page 56

Sachet Sew up a simple pouch, then fill with dried lavender for a special sachet that will keep your linens smelling fresh.

Motif 133 on page 82

Book Cover Embellish a book cover with a pretty floral motif—you may find yourself inspired to read more often!

Motif 92 on page 74

Blouse Embellish a linen blouse with a small floral motif.

Motif 189 on page 94

Lunch Bag Add a cute flower motif to your lunch bag for a touch of cheer.

Motif 95 on page 76

Greeting Card Stitch a seasonal flower motif, then transform it into a card to send to a friend.

Motif 122 on page 80

Oven Mitt Add a few fruit-themed motifs to customize your kitchen gear.

Motifs 238 and 239 on page 104

Sampler This spring flower sampler will brighten up any room.

Motifs 56–62 on page 68

Tools & Materials

EMBROIDERY FLOSS --

All of the designs in this book were created with No. 25 embroidery floss. This type of floss is composed of six strands that can be easily separated, allowing you to adjust the thickness. Olympus brand floss was used to stitch the designs in this book. A conversion chart for DMC brand is included on page 55.

No. 25 embroidery floss

Each skein of floss includes a label with a three- or four-digit color number. Metallic embroidery floss colors include an S before the color number. These numbers are used to represent the required floss color in the stitch diagram for each design.

Metallic embroidery floss

NEEDLES --

Use embroidery needles, which feature large eyes designed to accommodate embroidery floss. French embroidery needles are popular for their sharp tips that travel through a variety of fabrics with ease. Embroidery needles are available in several sizes, but sizes 3–7 should work for the designs in this book. Use the proper size needle based on the number of strands.

Remember, the higher the needle size, the smaller the needle!

Size 3

Size 5

Size 7

French embroidery needles

Needle Size	Number of Strands
No. 3	6
No. 5	3–4
No. 7	1–2

SCISSORS -

Use small thread snips to cut embroidery floss and fabric shears to cut embroidery fabric. Remember, sharp scissors make the job easier!

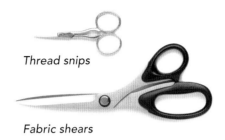

Thread snips

Fabric shears

FABRICS & HOOPS -

You can embroider just about any type of fabric, including cotton, linen, felt, and wool. For best results, look for a plain-woven fabric designed especially for embroidery.

Use an embroidery hoop to hold your fabric taut while stitching and prevent it from puckering. A 4–6 in (10–15 cm) hoop will work for most of the designs in this book.

Getting Started

HOW TO TRANSFER THE DESIGNS --------------------------------

1. Position dressmaker's carbon paper on your embroidery fabric with the chalk side down.

2. Copy the motif onto tracing paper. Align the tracing paper on top of the dressmaker's carbon paper. Position a sheet of cellophane on top.

3. Trace the motif using a stylus or ballpoint pen.

The cellophane isn't absolutely necessary, but it protects the tracing paper and makes the tracing process smoother.

4. The pressure of the pen will transfer the chalk onto the embroidery fabric in the outline of the motif.

HOW TO PREPARE EMBROIDERY FLOSS --------------------------

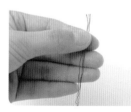

1. Hold the skein of embroidery floss with the label positioned between your fingers. Slowly pull one end.

2. Cut a 16–20 in (40–50 cm) long piece.

3. Separate the individual strands.

4. Realign the number of strands needed to stitch the design. Always separate the strands, even when using all six strands, as this practice prevents the thread from knotting.

HOW TO THREAD THE NEEDLE ------------------------------

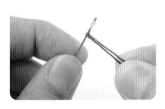   

1. Make a fold about 1 in (2.5 cm) from the end of the floss. Use your needle to apply pressure and create a crease.

2. Insert the fold through the eye of the needle.

3. Pull the folded end through the eye of the needle.

4. Position the needle about 4 in (10 cm) from the crease.

HOW TO MAKE KNOTS ------------------------------

TO START STITCHING

 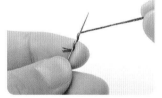  

1. Align the needle and the end of the floss.

2. Wrap the floss around the needle once or twice.

3. Hold the wraps between your fingers and pull the needle out. Move the wraps to the end of the floss to create a knot.

4. The knot is complete.

TO FINISH STITCHING

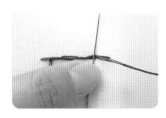 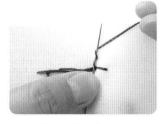 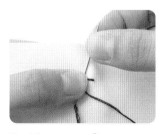 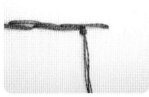

1. Align the needle on top of the stitches on the wrong side of the embroidery fabric.

2. Wrap the floss around the needle once or twice.

3. Use your finger to hold the wraps against the fabric and pull the needle out.

4. The knot is complete.

RIGHT SIDE VS. WRONG SIDE ------------------------------

The wrong side of your embroidery is just as important as the right side because it can influence the finished appearance of your work. Always start and finish your threads as shown on the previous page in order to produce neat, professional-looking finished designs.

When starting a new area of stitching, start a new thread or pass the needle under the back of other stitches to move to the new area, even if you're using the same color floss. This way, you'll avoid having long threads visible on the right side of your work. This is especially important when you're embroidering on light fabric.

The following photos show finished motifs as they appear on both the right and wrong sides.

Right Side   *Wrong Side*

EMBROIDERY FLOSS -

Since No. 25 embroidery floss is composed of six strands, you can separate the strands to adjust the thickness of your stitching. The following guide shows the different results that can be achieved by stitching with different numbers of strands.

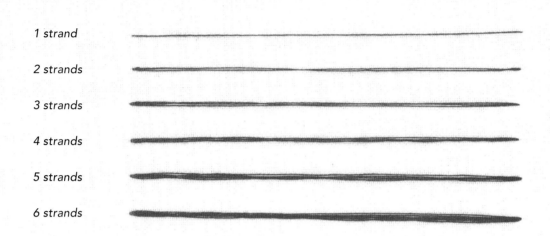

1 strand

2 strands

3 strands

4 strands

5 strands

6 strands

Altering the number of strands will influence the finished look of your stitches. The following examples show the different results than can be achieved by altering the number of strands of embroidery floss.

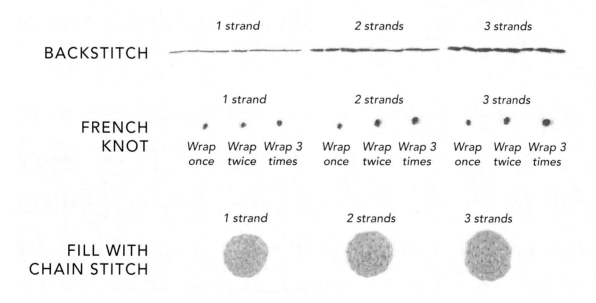

BACKSTITCH

1 strand 2 strands 3 strands

FRENCH KNOT

1 strand 2 strands 3 strands

Wrap once Wrap twice Wrap 3 times Wrap once Wrap twice Wrap 3 times Wrap once Wrap twice Wrap 3 times

FILL WITH CHAIN STITCH

1 strand 2 strands 3 strands

Embroidery Stitch Guide

All of the designs in this book were made with 15 basic embroidery stitches. The following guide illustrates how to make each stitch.

▶ STRAIGHT STITCH

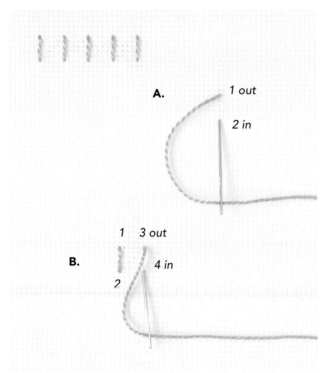

▶ RUNNING STITCH

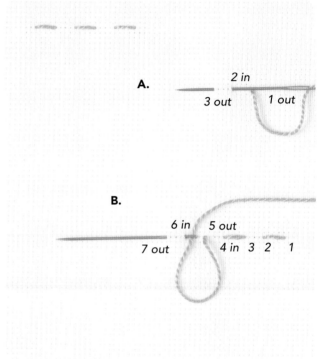

A. Draw the needle out at 1 and insert at 2. One straight stitch is complete.

B. To make the next stitch, draw the needle out at 3 and insert at 4.

A. Draw the needle out at 1. Insert at 2 and draw it out again at 3 in one movement.

B. Continue making a couple stitches at a time. Take care to keep the spacing consistent between stitches.

▶ BACKSTITCH

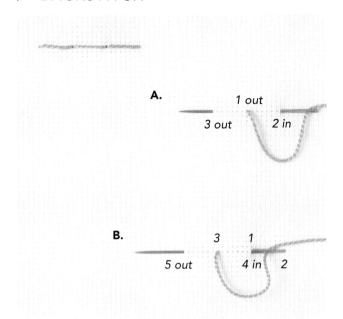

A. Draw the needle out at 1. Insert at 2, which is one stitch length behind 1. Draw the needle out again at 3, which is one stitch length ahead of 1.

B. To make the next stitch, insert the needle at 4, which is actually the same hole as 1. Draw the needle out again at 5, which is one stitch length ahead of 3.

▶ OUTLINE STITCH

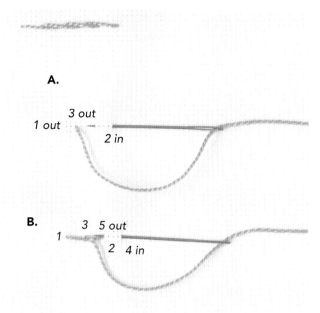

This stitch is worked from left to right.

A. Draw the needle out at 1. Insert the needle one stitch length away at 2, then draw the needle out again at 3, which is halfway between 1 and 2.

B. To make the next stitch, insert the needle one stitch length away at 4. Draw the needle out again at 5, which is halfway between 3 and 4.

▶ CHAIN STITCH

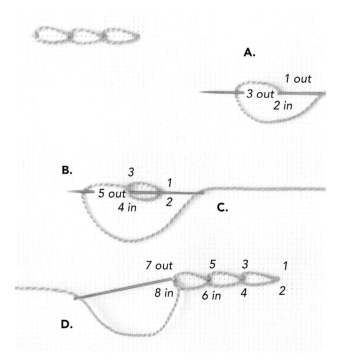

A. Draw the needle out at 1. Wrap the floss around the needle tip. Insert the needle at 2 (this is actually the same hole as 1), then draw the needle out again at 3.

B. Pull the needle and floss through the fabric until a small loop remains. The first chain is now complete. Insert the needle back through the same hole at 4.

C. Use the same process to draw the needle tip out at 5 and complete the next chain.

D. To finish a row of chain stitch, insert the needle back through the fabric, making a tiny straight stitch to secure the final chain, as shown by 8.

▶ FRENCH KNOT

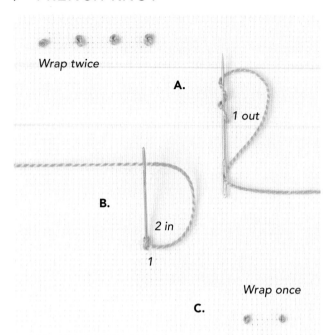

▶ LAZY DAISY STITCH

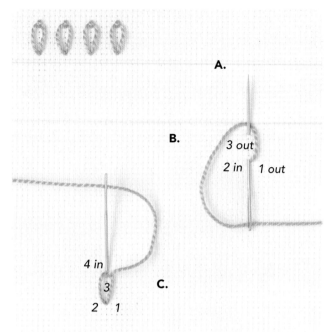

A. Draw the needle out at 1. Wrap the thread around the needle tip twice.

B. Insert the needle back through the fabric at 2, just next to 1. Hold the wraps against the fabric as you pull the needle and thread through the fabric to complete the knot.

C. For smaller French knots, wrap the thread around the needle only once.

A. Draw the needle out at 1. Wrap the floss around the needle tip. Insert the needle at 2 (this is actually the same hole as 1), then draw the needle out again at 3.

B. This is the same process used to make a chain stitch as shown on page 49.

C. Pull the needle and floss through the fabric until a small loop remains. Insert the needle at 4, making a tiny straight stitch to secure the loop.

▶ SATIN STITCH

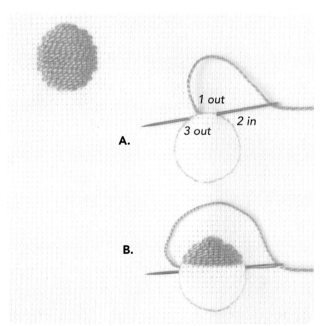

A. Draw the needle out at 1, insert it at 2, then draw the needle out again at 3.

B. Continue stitching from outline to outline to fill the area.

▶ LONG AND SHORT STITCH

▶ CROSS STITCH

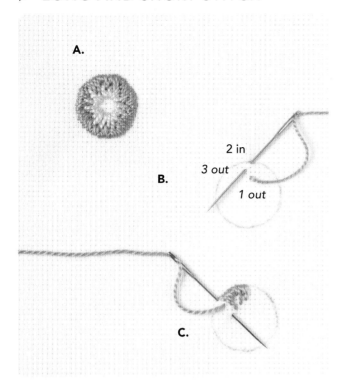

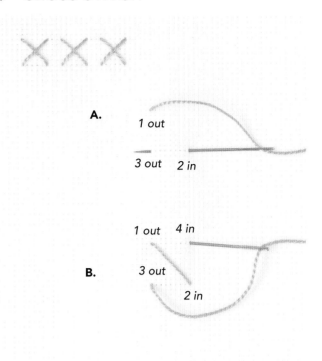

A. Draw the needle out at 1. Insert the needle at 2, then draw the needle out again at 3.

B. The distance from 2 to 3 should be shorter than the distance from 1 to 2.

C. Continue making both long and short stitches to fill the area.

It doesn't matter whether you cross the stitches from top to bottom or bottom to top, just be consistent throughout your work.

A. Draw the needle out at 1. Make a diagonal stitch and insert the needle at 2. Draw the needle out again at 3, which is parallel to 2.

B. Make another diagonal stitch to complete the cross and insert the needle at 4, which is parallel to 1.

▶ FISHBONE STITCH

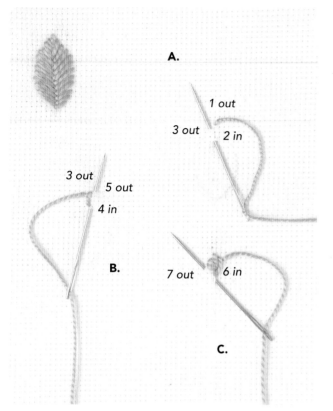

▶ BULLION KNOT

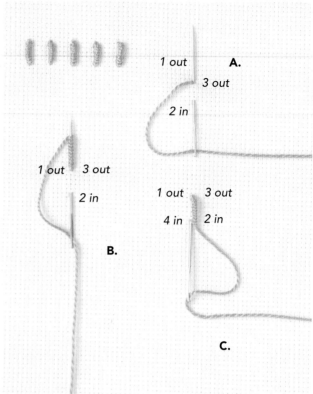

A. Draw the needle out at 1, which is at the tip of the design. Insert the needle at 2 in the center of the design. Draw the needle out at 3 along the left edge of the design.

B. Next, insert the needle at 4, which is adjacent to 2. Draw the needle out at 5 along the right edge of the design.

C. Insert the needle at 6, just beneath 4 and 5. Draw the needle out at 7. Continue working diagonal stitches from the center of the design.

A. Draw the needle out at 1 (this will be the top of the knot). Insert the needle at 2, then draw the needle out again at 3, which is actually the same hole as 1.

B. Wrap the floss around the tip of the needle as many times as directed. Hold the wraps against the fabric as you pull the needle out.

C. Insert the needle at 4, which is actually the same hole as 2, to secure the knot against the fabric.

▶ FLY STITCH

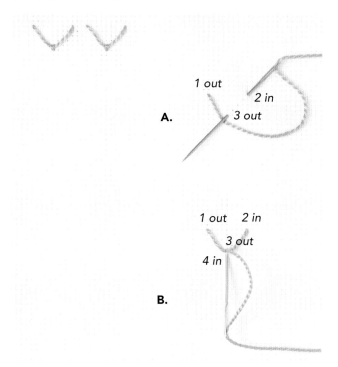

▶ BLANKET STITCH

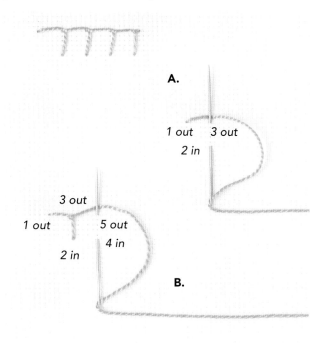

A. Draw the needle out at 1. Arrange the floss at a downward diagonal angle, then insert the needle at 2, which is parallel to 1. Draw the needle out at 3.

B. Pull the floss through the fabric to form a V-shaped stitch. Insert the needle at 4, directly beneath 3, to make a tiny straight stitch and secure the V in place.

A. Draw the needle out at 1. Arrange the floss so it extends to the right. Insert the needle at 2, then draw it out at 3, which is parallel to 1. Take care to keep the floss under the needle.

B. To make the next stitch, arrange the floss so it extends to the right, then insert the needle at 4, which is parallel to 2. Draw the needle out at 5, which is parallel to 1 and 3, taking care to keep the floss under the needle.

▶ COUCHING STITCH

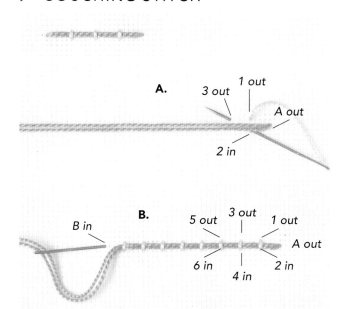

This example uses two different colors of floss to illustrate how to work the couching stitch. Refer to individual motif instructions for floss colors.

A. Draw the main floss color out at A, then arrange along the motif line. Draw the secondary floss color out at 1. Insert at 2, directly below 1, making a tiny straight stitch to secure the main floss in place. Draw the needle out at 3.

B. Continue making tiny, equally spaced straight stitches to secure the main floss in place along the motif line. To finish stitching, insert the main floss color back through the fabric at B.

How to Use This Book

Each motif in this book comes with a stitch guide, which includes all the information you'll need to stitch up the design, as well as a full-size template that can be traced easily. At the top of each page, you'll also find some general information that applies to all the motifs included on that page. The following guide explains how to read the embroidery diagrams.

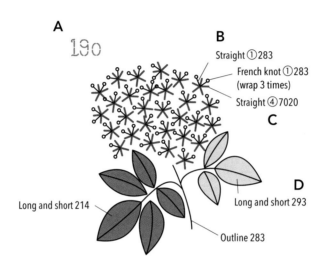

A

190

B

Straight ① 283

French knot ① 283
(wrap 3 times)

Straight ④ 7020

C

Long and short 214

Long and short 293

D

Outline 283

A. Motif Number: Use the motif number to locate your design. These numbers are also included on the photos of the stitched motifs at the beginning of the book.

B. Stitch Name: These labels indicate which stitch to use for each element of the design. Note: The word "stitch" is omitted from these labels in order to save space. Refer to the Embroidery Stitch Guide on pages 48–53 for instructions on making each of the 15 basic stitches used in this book.

C. Number of Strands: The circled numbers (for example: ②) indicate how many strands of embroidery floss to use when making a stitch.

D. Color Number: These numbers indicate the required floss color. Olympus brand floss was used to stitch the designs in this book. A conversion chart for DMC brand is included on page 55.

OLYMPUS	DMC	OLYMPUS	DMC	OLYMPUS	DMC	OLYMPUS	DMC	OLYMPUS	DMC	OLYMPUS	DMC
11	113	186	350	289	3346	543	307	733	742	1083	892
17	51	188	304	290	11	544	973	734	842	1084	891
22	93	190	326	291	727	546	444	735	422	1085	891
32	92	192	498	292	166	553	965	736	435	1119	899
36	57	196	814	293	370	554	741	737	433	1120	335
38	48	198	902	294	732	555	741	739	938	1121	309
61	105	202	503	303	518	556	740	742	842	1122	326
62	52	203	502	306	824	561	831	743	841	1205	3712
67	95	204	501	307	824	562	3046	745	839	1600	225
68	125	205	520	310	775	563	3045	751	945	1602	316
72	101	210	471	316	924	564	831	753	971	1603	221
100	819	212	471	318	939	565	830	754	970	1701	152
101	819	214	470	324	939	575	400	755	921	1702	758
102	818	216	470	341	927	580	728	758	920	1703	3328
103	776	218	469	342	926	581	973	765	225	1704	3350
104	3326	219	964	343	924	582	742	766	224	1705	347
105	894	220	959	352	3325	583	972	769	355	1706	347
106	893	221	993	353	334	600	554	782	758	1898	819
116	963	222	992	354	826	601	553	783	922	1900	818
117	776	223	958	356	312	602	553	784	922	1902	3687
119	3354	227	704	361	775	603	552	786	920	1904	3687
121	3687	228	704	362	800	604	552	792	225	1908	3685
122	3350	229	703	363	809	605	550	795	221	2011	470
124	605	231	702	369	828	611	3743	796	221	2013	469
125	604	235	471	384	807	612	3042	800	B5200	2016	935
126	603	236	470	385	806	613	28	801	BLANC	2020	3819
127	602	237	460	391	807	614	3041	810	762	2021	907
128	600	238	937	393	517	616	29	812	648	2022	911
131	3689	243	369	411	3024	621	211	813	3022	2023	3818
132	3688	244	368	412	648	622	210	815	611	2042	597
133	603	245	367	413	647	623	210	825	801	2050	522
134	718	246	501	414	646	624	209	841	822	2051	3363
135	917	247	319	415	645	625	208	842	613	2052	3363
136	915	251	504	423	3022	630	3742	843	612	2065	699
140	754	252	369	431	3023	631	3743	844	611	2070	3348
141	353	253	368	451	453	632	3042	845	611	2071	904
142	352	254	320	452	452	640	809	850	3865	2072	3850
143	351	255	501	485	318	642	794	900	310	2073	895
144	350	257	319	488	413	643	161	1014	899	2215	992
145	349	261	955	501	726	645	336	1026	350	2445	320
156	891	262	954	502	725	651	554	1027	347	2502	3812
161	225	263	913	503	977	653	208	1028	815	2835	832
163	224	264	911	516	782	654	597	1029	814	3042	415
165	223	265	909	520	745	655	550	1031	758	3043	930
166	223	273	3348	521	743	672	554	1032	3354	3052	3807
167	221	274	3347	522	956	673	553	1034	3350	3705	813
169	948	275	3346	523	741	675	552	1035	347	371A	996
170	353	276	3346	524	740	676	552	1042	605	3835	827
172	947	277	895	525	971	711	402	1043	604	5205	727
174	608	283	833	531	743	712	921	1044	893	6655	327
175	900	284	732	535	971	713	975	1045	893	7020	3866
180	754	285	830	540	746	721	677	1046	892	7025	3857
182	352	287	472	541	3078	723	729	1053	900	S106	E3821/5282
184	351	288	3012	542	445	731	712	1082	352		

Roses

Photos: Page 6

- ■ ◯ = Number of strands (use 2 strands, unless otherwise noted)
- ■ # = Color number
- ■ Wrap all French knots once, unless otherwise noted.

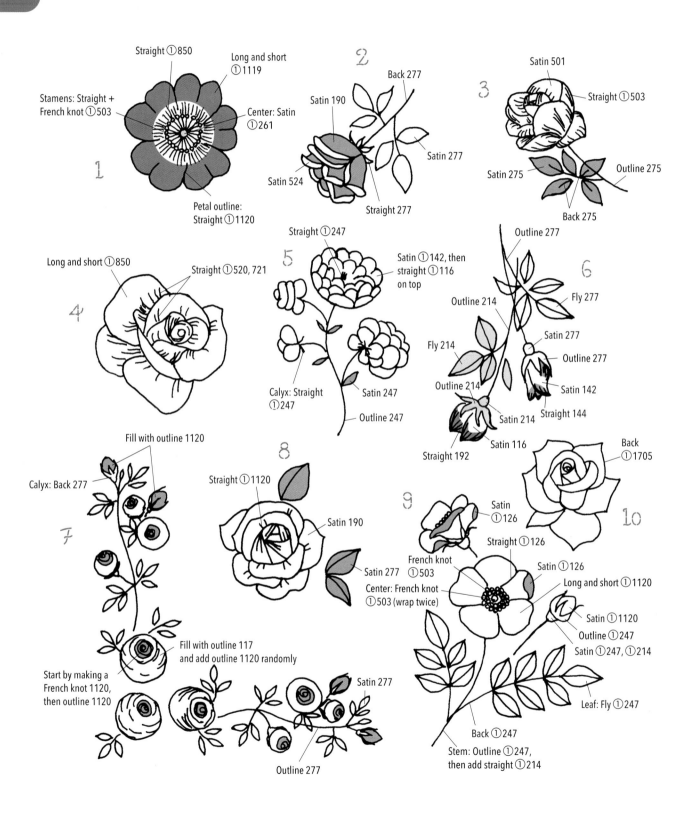

1
Straight ① 850
Long and short ① 1119
Stamens: Straight + French knot ① 503
Center: Satin ① 261
Petal outline: Straight ① 1120

2
Back 277
Satin 190
Satin 524
Straight 277
Satin 277

3
Satin 501
Straight ① 503
Satin 275
Back 275
Outline 275

4
Long and short ① 850
Straight ① 520, 721

5
Straight ① 247
Satin ① 142, then straight ① 116 on top
Calyx: Straight ① 247
Satin 247
Outline 247

6
Outline 277
Fly 277
Outline 214
Satin 277
Outline 277
Fly 214
Satin 142
Outline 214
Satin 214
Straight 144
Straight 192
Satin 116

7
Fill with outline 1120
Calyx: Back 277
Fill with outline 117 and add outline 1120 randomly
Start by making a French knot 1120, then outline 1120
Satin 277
Outline 277

8
Straight ① 1120
Satin 190
Satin 277

9
Satin ① 126
French knot ① 503
Center: French knot ① 503 (wrap twice)
Straight ① 126

10
Back ① 1705
Satin ① 126
Long and short ① 1120
Satin ① 1120
Outline ① 247
Satin ① 247, ① 214
Leaf: Fly ① 247
Back ① 247
Stem: Outline ① 247, then add straight ① 214

Roses

Photos: Page 7

- ■ ◯ = Number of strands (use 2 strands, unless otherwise noted)
- ■ # = Color number
- ■ Wrap all French knots once, unless otherwise noted.

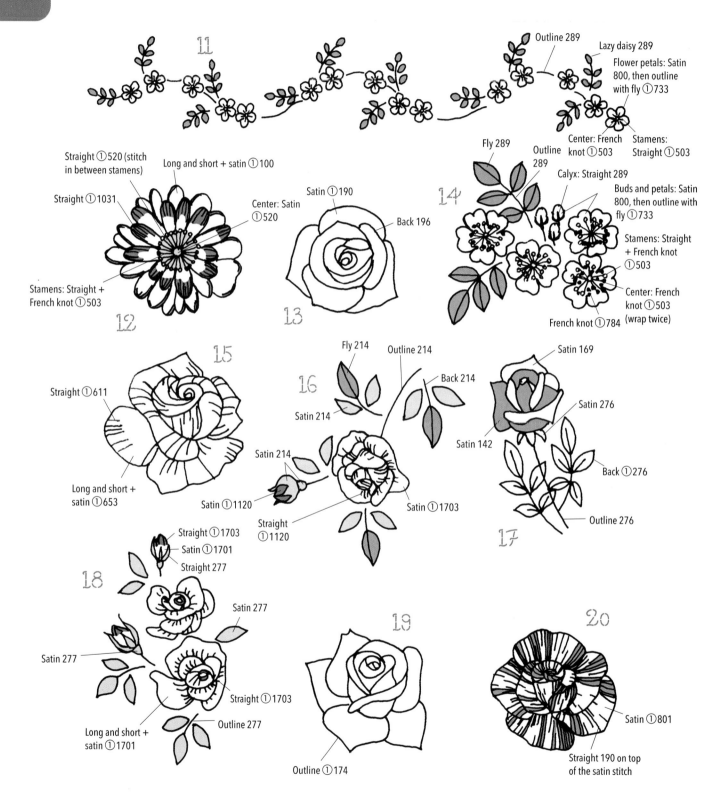

11

Outline 289

Lazy daisy 289

Flower petals: Satin 800, then outline with fly ①733

Fly 289

Outline 289

Center: French knot ①503

Stamens: Straight ①503

Straight ①520 (stitch in between stamens)

Long and short + satin ①100

Straight ①1031

Center: Satin ①520

Satin ①190

Back 196

14

Calyx: Straight 289

Buds and petals: Satin 800, then outline with fly ①733

Stamens: Straight + French knot ①503

Center: French knot ①503 (wrap twice)

French knot ①784

Stamens: Straight + French knot ①503

12

13

15

Straight ①611

Long and short + satin ①653

Fly 214

Outline 214

Back 214

16

Satin 214

Satin 214

Satin ①1120

Straight ①1120

Satin ①1703

Satin 169

Satin 276

Satin 142

Back ①276

Outline 276

17

18

Straight ①1703

Satin ①1701

Straight 277

Satin 277

Satin 277

Straight ①1703

Long and short + satin ①1701

Outline 277

19

Outline ①174

20

Satin ①801

Straight 190 on top of the satin stitch

Orchids & Chrysanthemums

Photos: Page 8

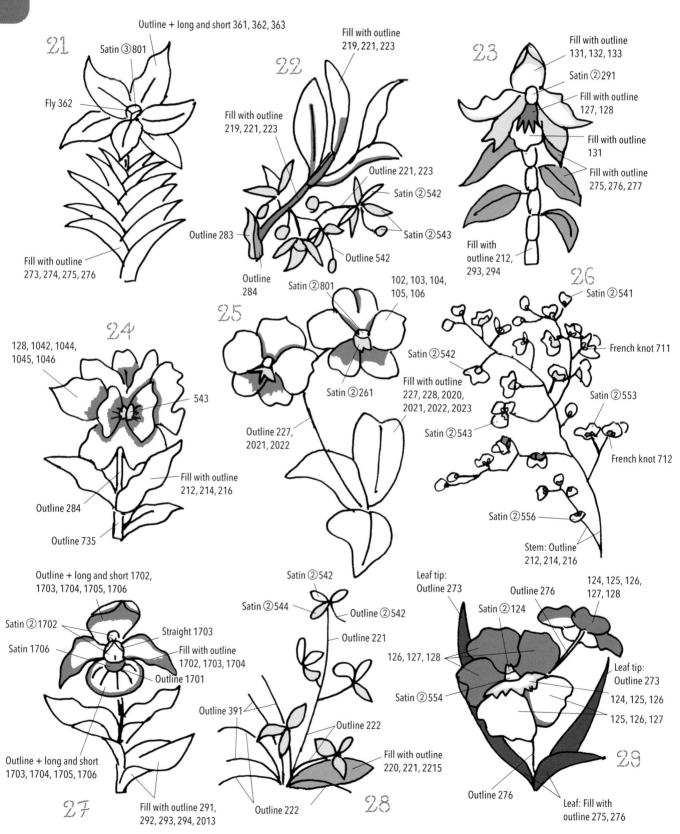

21

Satin ③ 801
Outline + long and short 361, 362, 363
Fly 362
Fill with outline 273, 274, 275, 276

22

Fill with outline 219, 221, 223
Fill with outline 219, 221, 223
Outline 221, 223
Satin ② 542
Satin ② 543
Outline 542
Outline 283
Outline 284

23

Fill with outline 131, 132, 133
Satin ② 291
Fill with outline 127, 128
Fill with outline 131
Fill with outline 275, 276, 277
Fill with outline 212, 293, 294

24

128, 1042, 1044, 1045, 1046
543
Outline 284
Outline 735
Fill with outline 212, 214, 216

25

Satin ② 801
102, 103, 104, 105, 106
Satin ② 261
Fill with outline 227, 228, 2020, 2021, 2022, 2023
Satin ② 543
Outline 227, 2021, 2022

26

Satin ② 541
French knot 711
Satin ② 553
French knot 712
Satin ② 556
Stem: Outline 212, 214, 216

27

Outline + long and short 1702, 1703, 1704, 1705, 1706
Satin ② 1702
Satin 1706
Straight 1703
Fill with outline 1702, 1703, 1704
Outline 1701
Outline + long and short 1703, 1704, 1705, 1706
Fill with outline 291, 292, 293, 294, 2013

28

Satin ② 542
Satin ② 544
Outline ② 542
Outline 221
Outline 391
Outline 222
Fill with outline 220, 221, 2215
Outline 222

29

Leaf tip: Outline 273
Outline 276
124, 125, 126, 127, 128
Satin ② 124
126, 127, 128
Satin ② 554
Leaf tip: Outline 273
124, 125, 126
125, 126, 127
Outline 276
Leaf: Fill with outline 275, 276

- ◼ ◯ = Number of strands (use 1 strand, unless otherwise noted)
- ◼ # = Color number
- ◼ Wrap all French knots twice, unless otherwise noted.
- ◼ When there are multiple color numbers listed, stitch in a gradation for shading.

21

22

23

24

25

26

27

28

29

Orchids & Chrysanthemums

Photos: Page 9

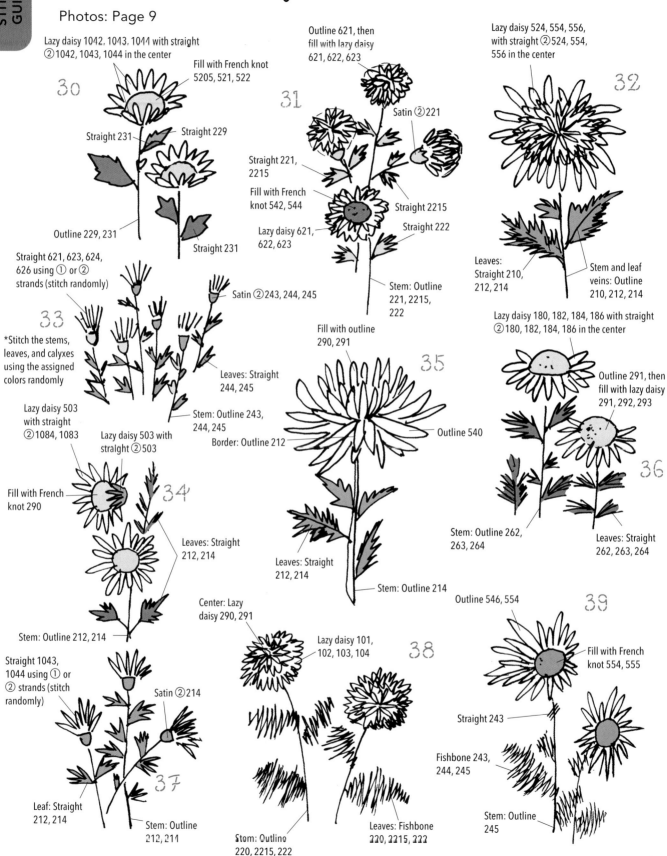

30 Lazy daisy 1042, 1043, 1044 with straight ②1042, 1043, 1044 in the center

Fill with French knot 5205, 521, 522

Straight 231

Straight 229

Outline 229, 231

Straight 231

33 Straight 621, 623, 624, 626 using ① or ② strands (stitch randomly)

*Stitch the stems, leaves, and calyxes using the assigned colors randomly

Satin ②243, 244, 245

Leaves: Straight 244, 245

Stem: Outline 243, 244, 245

34 Lazy daisy 503 with straight ②1084, 1083

Lazy daisy 503 with straight ②503

Fill with French knot 290

Leaves: Straight 212, 214

Stem: Outline 212, 214

Straight 1043, 1044 using ① or ② strands (stitch randomly)

Satin ②214

37 Leaf: Straight 212, 214

Stem: Outline 212, 214

31 Outline 621, then fill with lazy daisy 621, 622, 623

Satin ②221

Straight 221, 2215

Fill with French knot 542, 544

Lazy daisy 621, 622, 623

Straight 2215

Straight 222

Stem: Outline 221, 2215, 222

35 Fill with outline 290, 291

Outline 540

Border: Outline 212

Leaves: Straight 212, 214

Stem: Outline 214

Center: Lazy daisy 290, 291

38 Lazy daisy 101, 102, 103, 104

Stem: Outline 220, 2215, 222

Leaves: Fishbone 220, 2215, 222

32 Lazy daisy 524, 554, 556, with straight ②524, 554, 556 in the center

Leaves: Straight 210, 212, 214

Stem and leaf veins: Outline 210, 212, 214

Lazy daisy 180, 182, 184, 186 with straight ②180, 182, 184, 186 in the center

Outline 291, then fill with lazy daisy 291, 292, 293

36 Stem: Outline 262, 263, 264

Leaves: Straight 262, 263, 264

39 Outline 546, 554

Fill with French knot 554, 555

Straight 243

Fishbone 243, 244, 245

Stem: Outline 245

- ■ ⬤ ◯ = Number of strands (use 1 strand, unless otherwise noted)
- ■ # = Color number
- ■ Wrap all French knots twice, unless otherwise noted.
- ■ When there are multiple color numbers listed, stitch in a gradation for shading.

Spring Flowers

Photos: Page 10

■ ○ = Number of strands (use 2 strands, unless otherwise noted)
■ # = Color number
■ Wrap all French knots twice, unless otherwise noted.

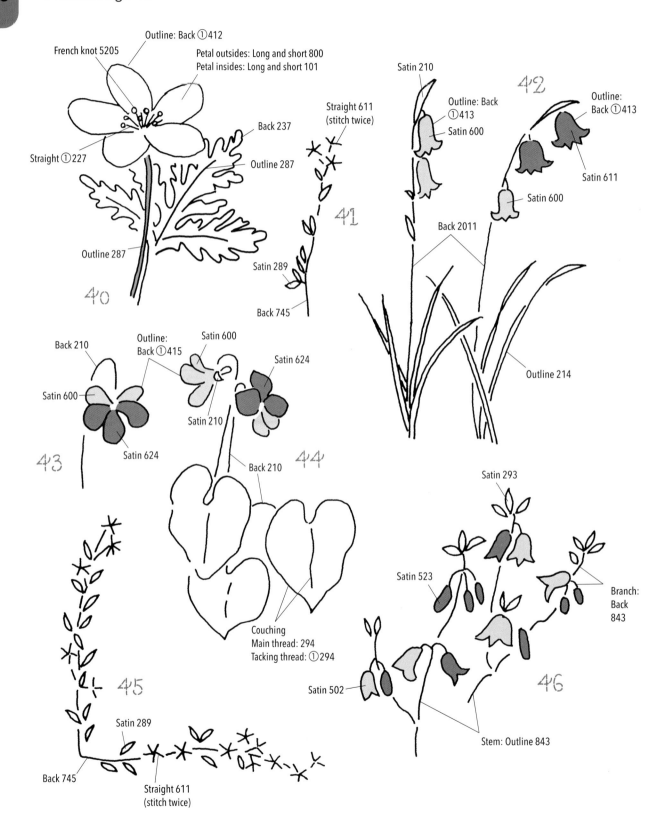

40
French knot 5205
Outline: Back ①412
Petal outsides: Long and short 800
Petal insides: Long and short 101
Straight ①227
Back 237
Outline 287
Outline 287

41
Straight 611 (stitch twice)
Satin 289
Back 745

42
Satin 210
Outline: Back ①413
Satin 600
Outline: Back ①413
Satin 611
Satin 600
Back 2011
Outline 214

43
Back 210
Outline: Back ①415
Satin 600
Satin 600
Satin 210
Satin 624
Satin 624

44
Satin 624
Back 210
Couching
Main thread: 294
Tacking thread: ①294

45
Satin 289
Back 745
Straight 611 (stitch twice)

46
Satin 293
Satin 523
Satin 502
Stem: Outline 843
Branch: Back 843

Spring Flowers

Photos: Page 11

- ■ ○ = Number of strands (use 2 strands, unless otherwise noted)
- ■ # = Color number
- ■ Wrap all French knots twice, unless otherwise noted.

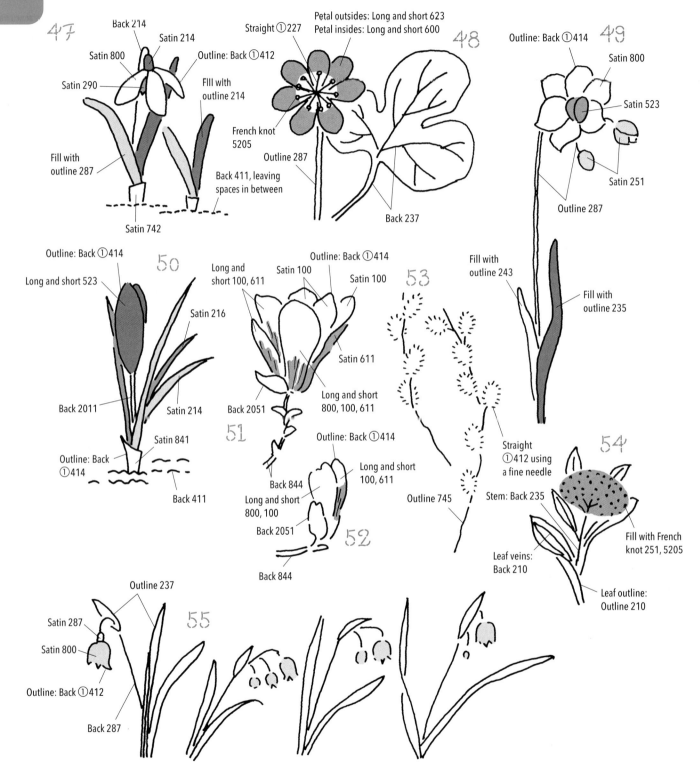

47

Back 214
Satin 214
Satin 800
Satin 290
Outline: Back ①412
Fill with outline 214
Fill with outline 287
Satin 742

48

Straight ①227
Petal outsides: Long and short 623
Petal insides: Long and short 600
French knot 5205
Outline 287
Back 411, leaving spaces in between
Back 237

49

Outline: Back ①414
Satin 800
Satin 523
Satin 251
Outline 287
Fill with outline 243
Fill with outline 235

50

Outline: Back ①414
Long and short 523
Satin 216
Satin 214
Back 2011
Satin 841
Outline: Back ①414
Back 411

51

Long and short 100, 611
Satin 100
Outline: Back ①414
Satin 100
Satin 611
Long and short 800, 100, 611
Back 2051
Long and short 800, 100
Back 2051
Back 844

52

Outline: Back ①414
Long and short 100, 611
Back 844

53

Outline 745

54

Straight ①412 using a fine needle
Stem: Back 235
Fill with French knot 251, 5205
Leaf veins: Back 210
Leaf outline: Outline 210

55

Outline 237
Satin 287
Satin 800
Outline: Back ①412
Back 287

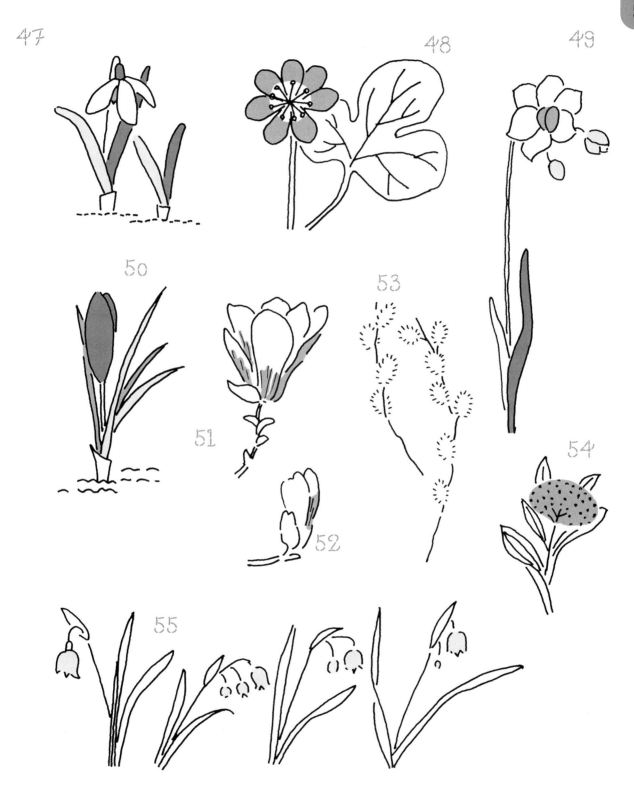

47

48

49

50

53

51

52

54

55

Spring Flowers

Photos: Page 12

- ■ ○ = Number of strands (use 2 strands, unless otherwise noted)
- ■ # = Color number
- ■ Wrap all French knots twice, unless otherwise noted.

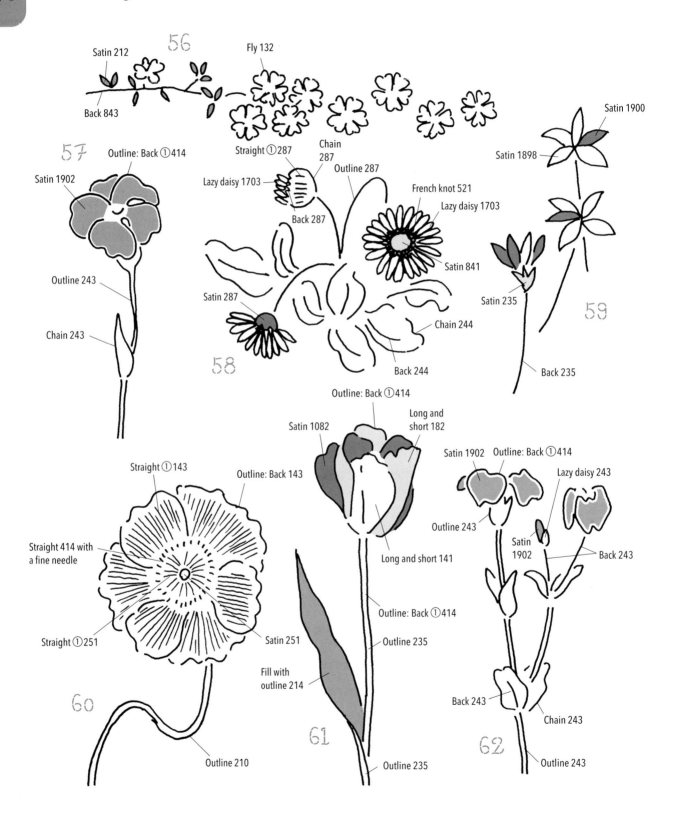

56
Satin 212
Back 843
Fly 132

57
Outline: Back ①414
Satin 1902
Straight ①287
Lazy daisy 1703
Chain 287
Outline 287
Back 287
French knot 521
Lazy daisy 1703
Satin 841
Satin 287
Chain 244
Back 244
Outline 243
Chain 243

58

Satin 1900
Satin 1898
59
Satin 235
Back 235

60
Straight ①143
Outline: Back 143
Straight 414 with a fine needle
Straight ①251
Satin 251
Outline 210

61
Outline: Back ①414
Satin 1082
Long and short 182
Long and short 141
Outline: Back ①414
Outline 235
Fill with outline 214
Outline 235

62
Satin 1902
Outline: Back ①414
Lazy daisy 243
Outline 243
Satin 1902
Back 243
Back 243
Chain 243
Outline 243

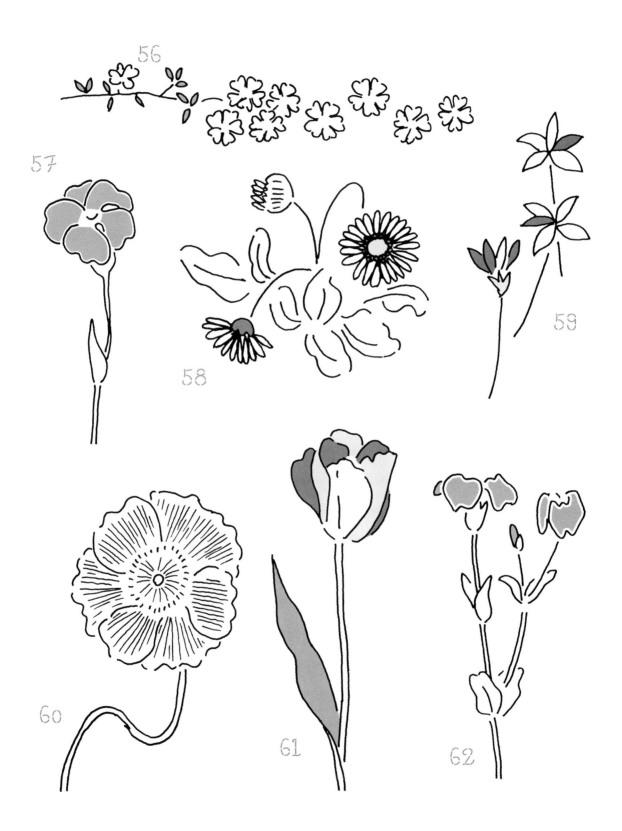

Spring Flowers

Photos: Page 13

- ■ ○ = Number of strands (use 2 strands, unless otherwise noted)
- ■ # = Color number
- ■ Wrap all French knots twice, unless otherwise noted.

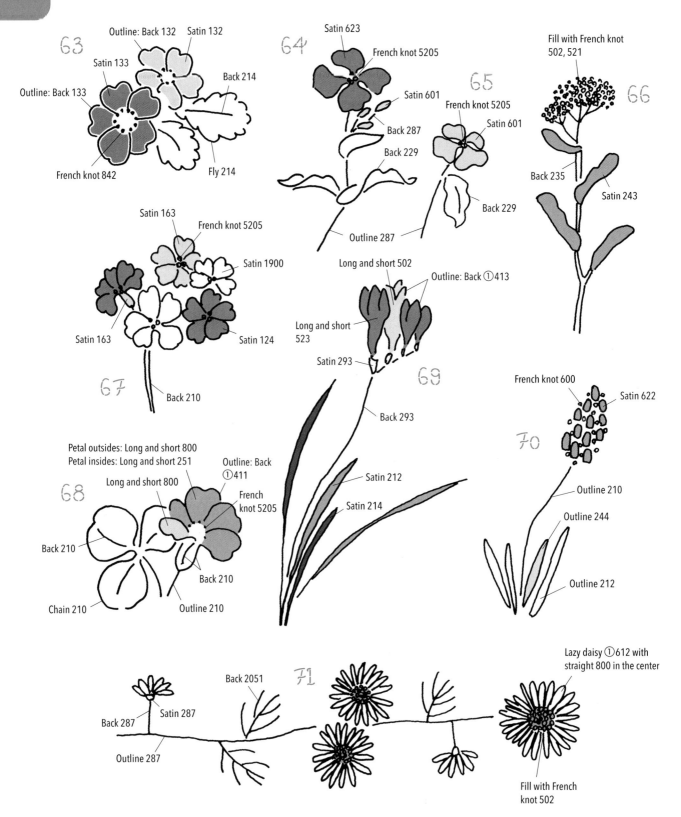

63
- Outline: Back 132
- Satin 132
- Satin 133
- Outline: Back 133
- Back 214
- French knot 842
- Fly 214

64
- Satin 623
- French knot 5205
- Satin 601
- Back 287
- Back 229
- Outline 287

65
- French knot 5205
- Satin 601
- Back 229

66
- Fill with French knot 502, 521
- Back 235
- Satin 243

67
- Satin 163
- French knot 5205
- Satin 1900
- Satin 163
- Satin 124
- Back 210

68
- Petal outsides: Long and short 800
- Petal insides: Long and short 251
- Long and short 800
- Outline: Back ①411
- French knot 5205
- Back 210
- Back 210
- Chain 210
- Outline 210

69
- Long and short 502
- Outline: Back ①413
- Long and short 523
- Satin 293
- Back 293
- Satin 212
- Satin 214

70
- French knot 600
- Satin 622
- Outline 210
- Outline 244
- Outline 212

71
- Back 287
- Satin 287
- Outline 287
- Back 2051
- Lazy daisy ①612 with straight 800 in the center
- Fill with French knot 502

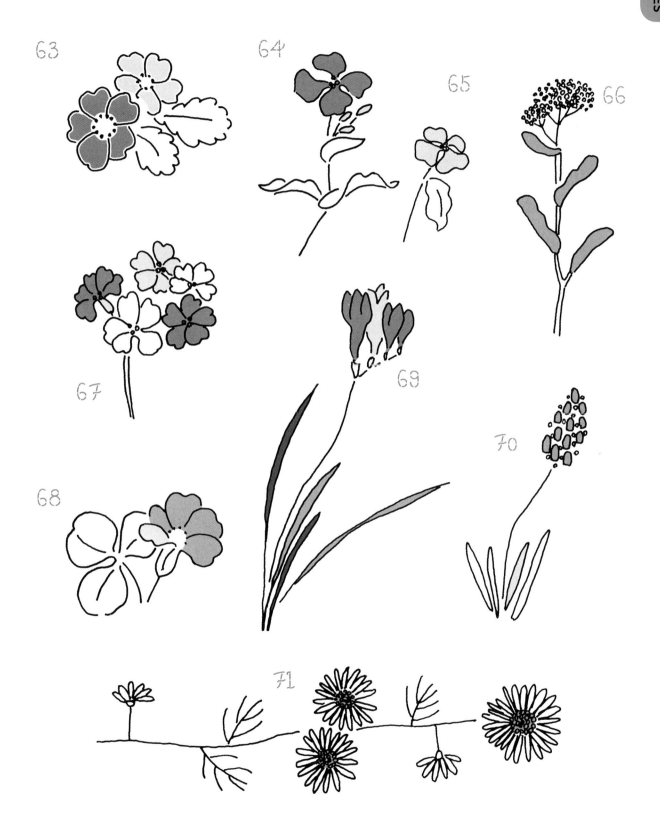

63
64
65
66
67
68
69
70
71

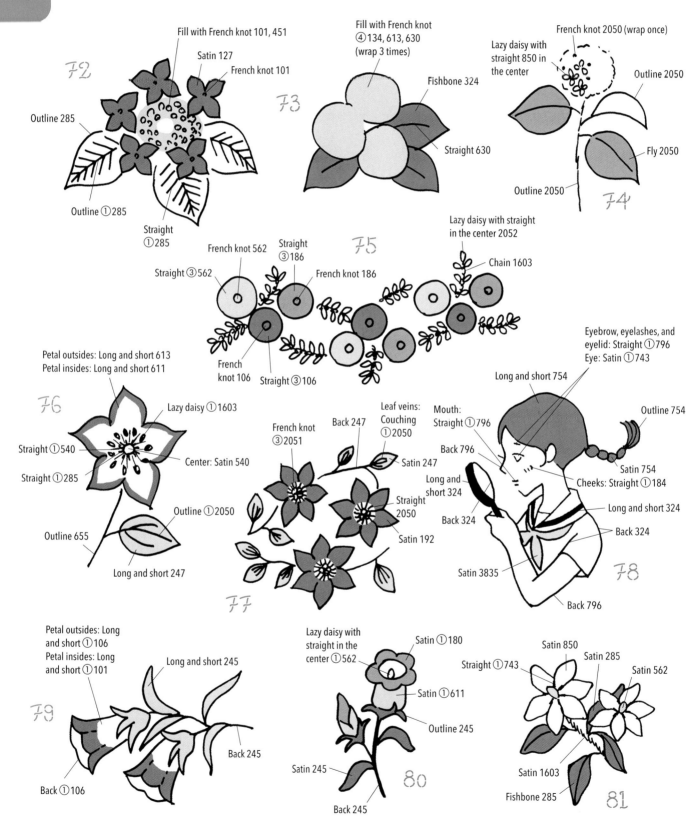

Summer Flowers

Photos: Page 14

- ■ ○ = Number of strands (use 2 strands, unless otherwise noted)
- ■ # = Color number
- ■ Wrap all French knots twice, unless otherwise noted.

72

Fill with French knot 101, 451
Satin 127
French knot 101
Outline 285
Outline ①285
Straight ①285

73

Fill with French knot ④134, 613, 630 (wrap 3 times)
Fishbone 324
Straight 630

74

French knot 2050 (wrap once)
Lazy daisy with straight 850 in the center
Outline 2050
Fly 2050
Outline 2050

75

French knot 562
Straight ③562
Straight ③186
French knot 186
Lazy daisy with straight in the center 2052
Chain 1603
French knot 106
Straight ③106

76

Petal outsides: Long and short 613
Petal insides: Long and short 611
Lazy daisy ①1603
Straight ①540
Center: Satin 540
Straight ①285
Outline ①2050
Outline 655
Long and short 247

77

French knot ③2051
Back 247
Leaf veins: Couching ①2050
Satin 247
Straight 2050
Satin 192

78

Eyebrow, eyelashes, and eyelid: Straight ①796
Eye: Satin ①743
Long and short 754
Mouth: Straight ①796
Back 796
Outline 754
Long and short 324
Satin 754
Cheeks: Straight ①184
Back 324
Long and short 324
Back 324
Satin 3835
Back 796

79

Petal outsides: Long and short ①106
Petal insides: Long and short ①101
Long and short 245
Back 245
Back ①106

80

Lazy daisy with straight in the center ①562
Satin ①180
Satin ①611
Outline 245
Satin 245
Back 245

81

Satin 850
Straight ①743
Satin 285
Satin 562
Satin 1603
Fishbone 285

Summer Flowers

Photos: Page 15

- ■ ○ = Number of strands (use 2 strands, unless otherwise noted)
- ■ # = Color number
- ■ Wrap all French knots twice, unless otherwise noted.

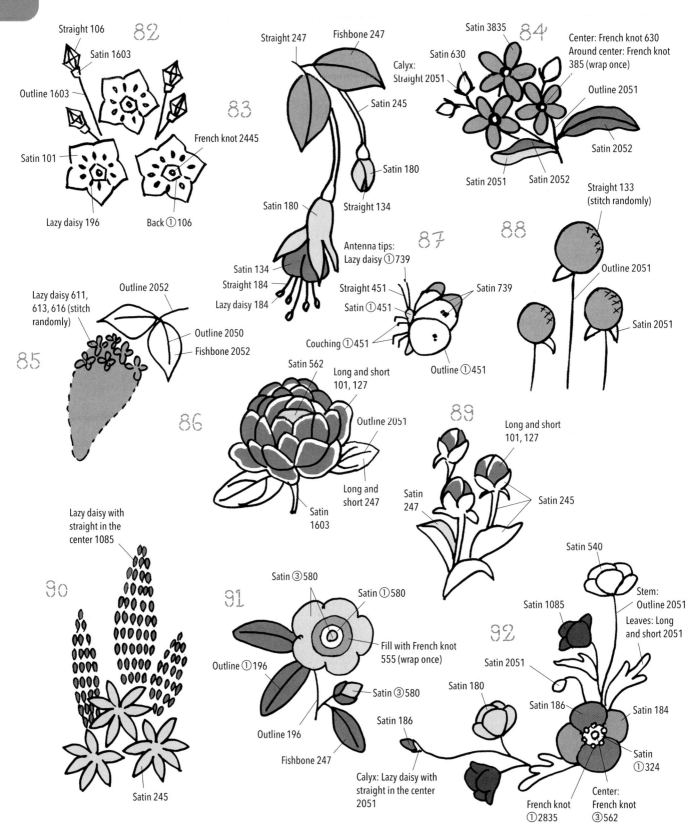

82
Straight 106
Satin 1603
Outline 1603
Satin 101
Lazy daisy 196
Back ①106
French knot 2445

83
Straight 247
Fishbone 247
Calyx: Straight 2051
Satin 245
Satin 180
Straight 134
Satin 180
Satin 134
Straight 184
Lazy daisy 184

84
Satin 3835
Satin 630
Center: French knot 630
Around center: French knot 385 (wrap once)
Outline 2051
Satin 2052
Satin 2051
Satin 2052

88
Straight 133 (stitch randomly)
Outline 2051
Satin 2051

85
Lazy daisy 611, 613, 616 (stitch randomly)
Outline 2052
Outline 2050
Fishbone 2052

86
Satin 562
Long and short 101, 127
Outline 2051
Long and short 247
Satin 1603

87
Antenna tips: Lazy daisy ①739
Satin 739
Straight 451
Satin ①451
Couching ①451
Outline ①451

89
Long and short 101, 127
Satin 247
Satin 245

90
Lazy daisy with straight in the center 1085
Satin 245

91
Satin ③580
Satin ①580
Fill with French knot 555 (wrap once)
Outline ①196
Satin ③580
Outline 196
Satin 186
Fishbone 247
Calyx: Lazy daisy with straight in the center 2051

92
Satin 540
Stem: Outline 2051
Leaves: Long and short 2051
Satin 1085
Satin 2051
Satin 180
Satin 186
Satin 184
Satin ①324
Center: French knot ③562
French knot ①2835

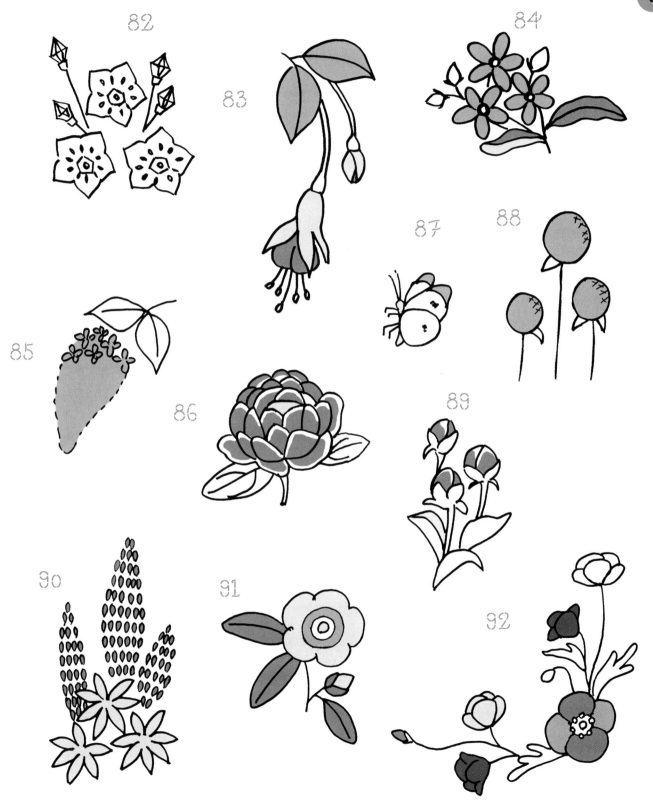

82

83

84

87

88

85

86

89

90

91

92

Summer Flowers

Photos: Page 16

■ ○ = Number of strands (use 2 strands, unless otherwise noted)
■ # = Color number
■ Wrap all French knots twice, unless otherwise noted.

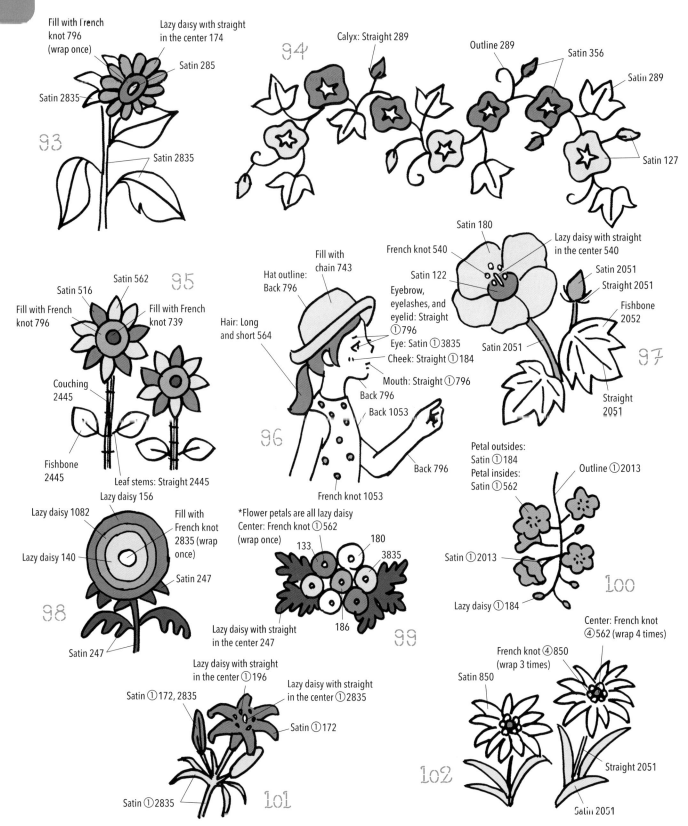

93

Fill with French knot 796 (wrap once)

Lazy daisy with straight in the center 174

Satin 285

Satin 2835

Satin 2835

94

Calyx: Straight 289

Outline 289

Satin 356

Satin 289

Satin 127

95

Satin 562

Satin 516

Fill with French knot 796

Fill with French knot 739

Couching 2445

Fishbone 2445

Leaf stems: Straight 2445

96

Fill with chain 743

Hat outline: Back 796

Hair: Long and short 564

French knot 540

Satin 122

Eyebrow, eyelashes, and eyelid: Straight ①796

Eye: Satin ①3835

Cheek: Straight ①184

Mouth: Straight ①796

Back 796

Back 1053

Back 796

French knot 1053

97

Satin 180

Lazy daisy with straight in the center 540

Satin 2051

Straight 2051

Fishbone 2052

Satin 2051

Straight 2051

98

Lazy daisy 156

Lazy daisy 1082

Lazy daisy 140

Fill with French knot 2835 (wrap once)

Satin 247

Satin 247

99

*Flower petals are all lazy daisy
Center: French knot ①562 (wrap once)

133

180

3835

186

Lazy daisy with straight in the center 247

100

Petal outsides: Satin ①184
Petal insides: Satin ①562

Outline ①2013

Satin ①2013

Lazy daisy ①184

101

Lazy daisy with straight in the center ①196

Lazy daisy with straight in the center ①2835

Satin ①172, 2835

Satin ①172

Satin ①2835

102

Center: French knot ④562 (wrap 4 times)

French knot ④850 (wrap 3 times)

Satin 850

Straight 2051

Satin 2051

Summer Flowers

Photos: Page 17

- ■ ○ = Number of strands (use 2 strands, unless otherwise noted)
- ■ # = Color number
- ■ Wrap all French knots once, unless otherwise noted.

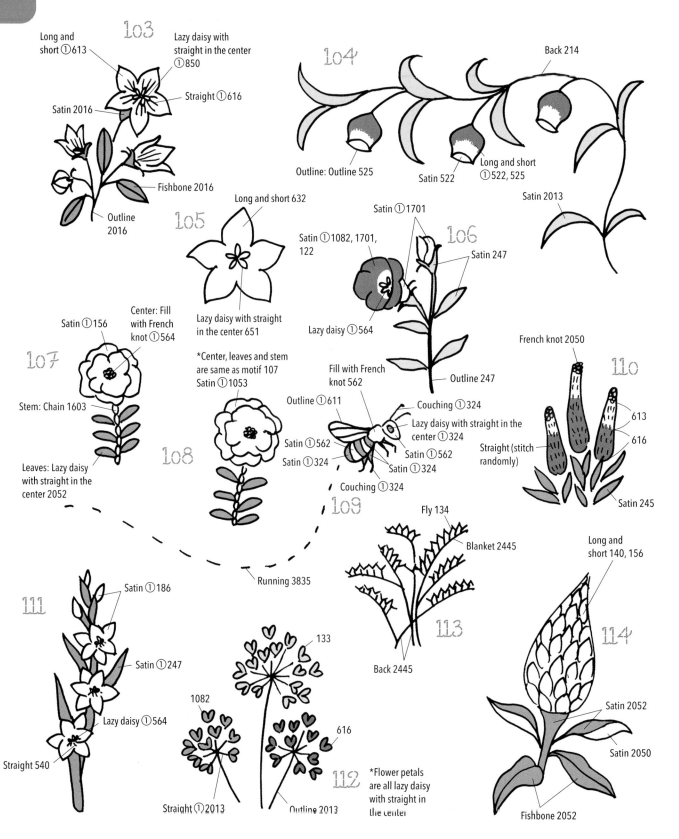

103
Long and short ①613
Lazy daisy with straight in the center ①850
Straight ①616
Satin 2016
Fishbone 2016
Outline 2016

104
Back 214
Outline: Outline 525
Satin 522
Long and short ①522, 525
Satin 2013

105
Long and short 632
Lazy daisy with straight in the center 651

106
Satin ①1701
Satin ①1082, 1701, 122
Satin 247
Lazy daisy ①564
Outline 247

107
Satin ①156
Center: Fill with French knot ①564
Stem: Chain 1603
Leaves: Lazy daisy with straight in the center 2052

108
*Center, leaves and stem are same as motif 107
Satin ①1053

Fill with French knot 562
Outline ①611
Couching ①324
Lazy daisy with straight in the center ①324
Satin ①562
Satin ①324
Satin ①562
Satin ①324
Couching ①324

109
Running 3835

110
French knot 2050
613
616
Straight (stitch randomly)
Satin 245

111
Satin ①186
Satin ①247
Lazy daisy ①564
Straight 540

112
133
1082
616
Straight ①2013
Outline 2013
*Flower petals are all lazy daisy with straight in the center

113
Fly 134
Blanket 2445
Back 2445

114
Long and short 140, 156
Satin 2052
Satin 2050
Fishbone 2052

103

104

105

106

107

108

109

110

111

112

113

114

Autumn & Winter Flowers

Photos: Page 18

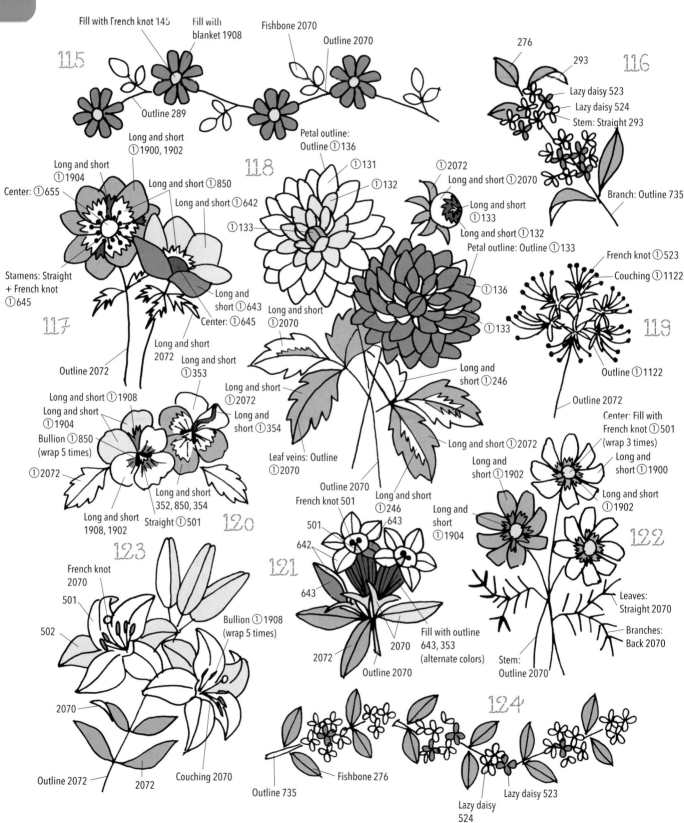

115 — Fill with French knot 145 · Fill with blanket 1908 · Fishbone 2070 · Outline 2070 · Outline 289

116 — 276 · 293 · Lazy daisy 523 · Lazy daisy 524 · Stem: Straight 293 · Branch: Outline 735

117 — Long and short ①1900, 1902 · Long and short ①1904 · Center: ①655 · Long and short ①850 · Long and short ①642 · Stamens: Straight + French knot ①645 · Long and short ①643 · Center: ①645 · Outline 2072 · Long and short 2072

118 — Petal outline: Outline ①136 · ①131 · ①132 · ①133 · ①2072 · Long and short ①2070 · Long and short ①133 · Long and short ①132 · Petal outline: Outline ①133 · ①136 · ①133 · Long and short ①2070 · Long and short ①353 · Long and short ①2072 · Long and short ①354 · Long and short ①246 · Long and short ①2072 · Leaf veins: Outline ①2070

119 — French knot ①523 · Couching ①1122 · Outline ①1122 · Outline 2072

120 — Long and short ①1908 · Long and short ①1904 · Bullion ①850 (wrap 5 times) · ①2072 · Long and short 352, 850, 354 · Long and short 1908, 1902 · Straight ①501

121 — Outline 2070 · French knot 501 · Long and short ①246 643 · 501 · 642 · 643 · 2070 · Fill with outline 643, 353 (alternate colors) · 2072 · Outline 2070 · Long and short ①1904

122 — Center: Fill with French knot ①501 (wrap 3 times) · Long and short ①1900 · Long and short ①1902 · Long and short ①1902 · Leaves: Straight 2070 · Branches: Back 2070 · Stem: Outline 2070

123 — French knot 2070 · 501 · 502 · Bullion ①1908 (wrap 5 times) · 2070 · Outline 2072 · 2072 · Couching 2070

124 — Fishbone 276 · Outline 735 · Lazy daisy 523 · Lazy daisy 524

80 PLANT LADY EMBROIDERY

- ■ ○ = Number of strands (use 2 strands, unless otherwise noted)
- ■ # = Color number
- ■ Use satin stitch, unless otherwise noted.
- ■ Wrap all French knots twice, unless otherwise noted.

Autumn & Winter Flowers

Photos: Page 19

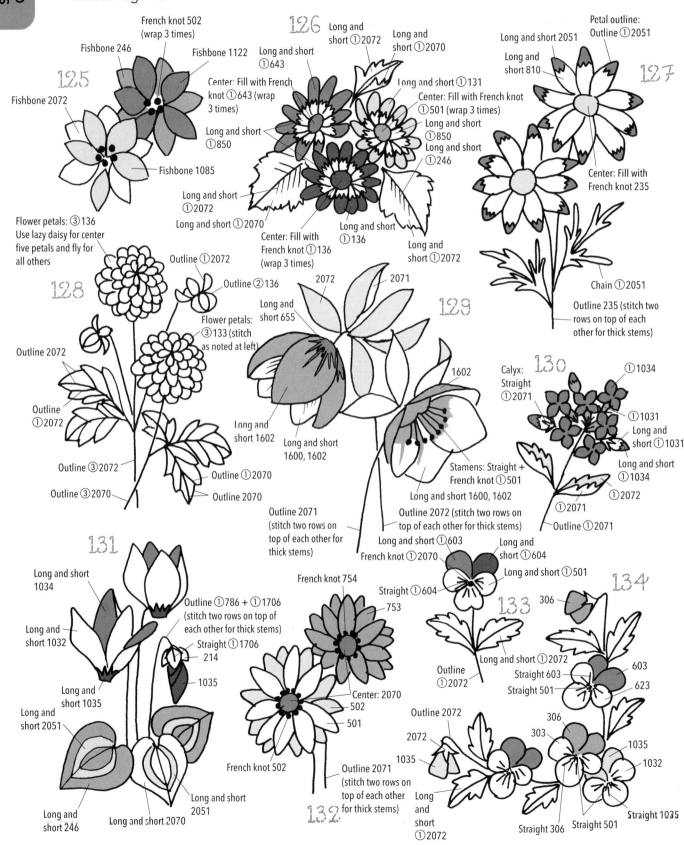

125

Fishbone 246

Fishbone 2072

French knot 502 (wrap 3 times)

Fishbone 1122

Fishbone 1085

Flower petals: ③136
Use lazy daisy for center five petals and fly for all others

126

Long and short ①2072

Long and short ①2070

Long and short ①643

Center: Fill with French knot ①643 (wrap 3 times)

Long and short ①850

Long and short ①131

Center: Fill with French knot ①501 (wrap 3 times)

Long and short ①850

Long and short ①246

Long and short ①2072

Long and short ①2070

Center: Fill with French knot ①136 (wrap 3 times)

Long and short ①136

Long and short ①2072

127

Petal outline: Outline ①2051

Long and short 2051

Long and short 810

Center: Fill with French knot 235

Chain ①2051

Outline 235 (stitch two rows on top of each other for thick stems)

128

Outline ①2072

Outline ②136

Flower petals: ③133 (stitch as noted at left)

Outline 2072

Outline ①2072

Outline ③2072

Outline ③2070

Outline ①2070

Outline 2070

129

2072

2071

Long and short 655

Long and short 1602

Long and short 1600, 1602

Outline 2071 (stitch two rows on top of each other for thick stems)

1602

Stamens: Straight + French knot ①501

Long and short 1600, 1602

Outline 2072 (stitch two rows on top of each other for thick stems)

Long and short ①603

French knot ①2070

130

Calyx: Straight ①2071

①1034

①1031

Long and short ①1031

Long and short ①1034

②2072

①2071

Outline ①2071

131

Long and short 1034

Long and short 1032

Long and short 1035

Long and short 2051

Long and short 246

Long and short 2070

Long and short 2051

Outline ①786 + ①1706 (stitch two rows on top of each other for thick stems)

Straight ①1706

214

1035

132

French knot 754

753

Center: 2070

502

501

French knot 502

Outline 2071 (stitch two rows on top of each other for thick stems)

Long and short ①2072

Long and short ①604

Straight ①604

Long and short ①501

133

306

Outline ①2072

Outline 2072

2072

1035

Long and short ①2072

Straight 603

Straight 501

Straight 306

Straight 501

134

603

623

306

303

1035

1032

Straight 1035

- ○ = Number of strands (use 2 strands, unless otherwise noted)
- # = Color number
- Use satin stitch, unless otherwise noted.
- Wrap all French knots twice, unless otherwise noted.

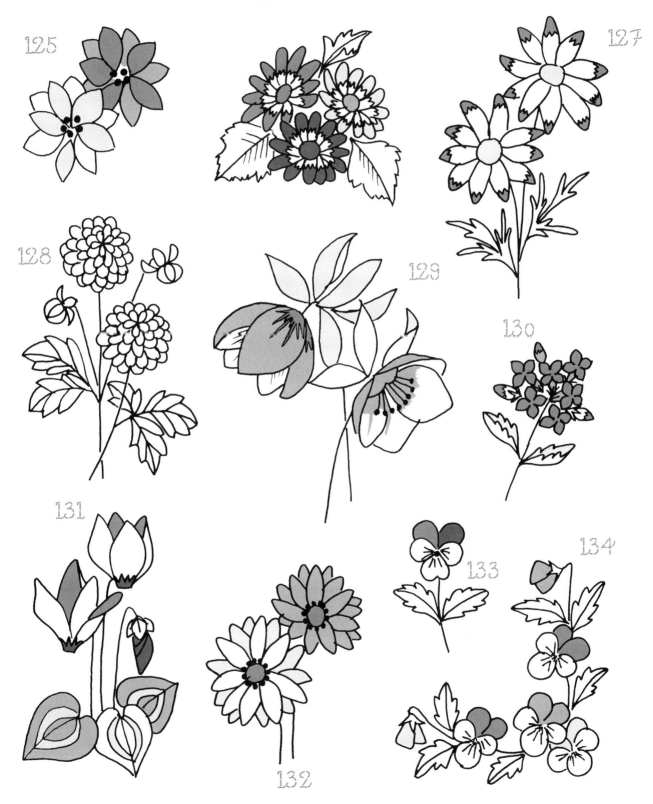

Flower Branches

- ■ ○ = Number of strands (use 2 strands, unless otherwise noted)
- ■ # = Color number
- ■ Wrap all French knots once, unless otherwise noted.

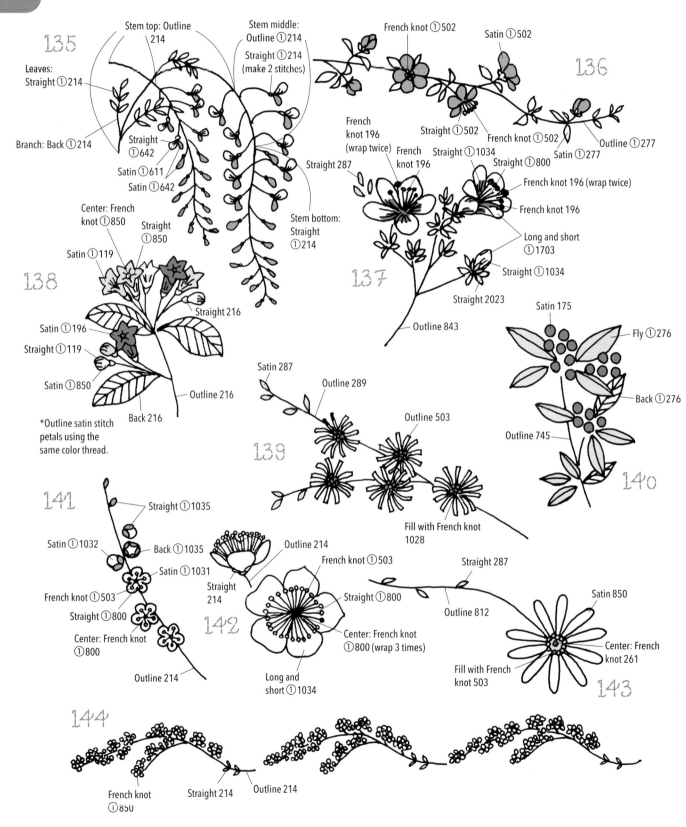

135

Stem top: Outline ①214

Leaves: Straight ①214

Branch: Back ①214

Straight ①642

Satin ①611

Satin ①642

Stem middle: Outline ①214

Straight ①214 (make 2 stitches)

Center: French knot ①850

Straight ①850

Satin ①119

138

Satin ①196

Straight ①119

Satin ①850

Straight 216

Outline 216

Back 216

*Outline satin stitch petals using the same color thread.

Stem bottom: Straight ①214

136

French knot ①502

Satin ①502

Straight ①502

French knot ①502

Outline ①277

Satin ①277

French knot 196 (wrap twice)

Straight 287

French knot 196

French knot ①503

137

Straight ①1034

Straight ①800

French knot 196 (wrap twice)

French knot 196

Long and short ①1703

Straight ①1034

Straight 2023

Outline 843

Satin 175

Fly ①276

Back ①276

Outline 745

140

Satin 287

Outline 289

Outline 503

139

Fill with French knot 1028

141

Straight ①1035

Satin ①1032

Back ①1035

Satin ①1031

French knot ①503

Straight ①800

Center: French knot ①800

Outline 214

Outline 214

Straight 214

142

French knot ①503

Straight ①800

Center: French knot ①800 (wrap 3 times)

Long and short ①1034

Straight 287

Outline 812

Fill with French knot 503

Satin 850

Center: French knot 261

143

144

French knot ①850

Straight 214

Outline 214

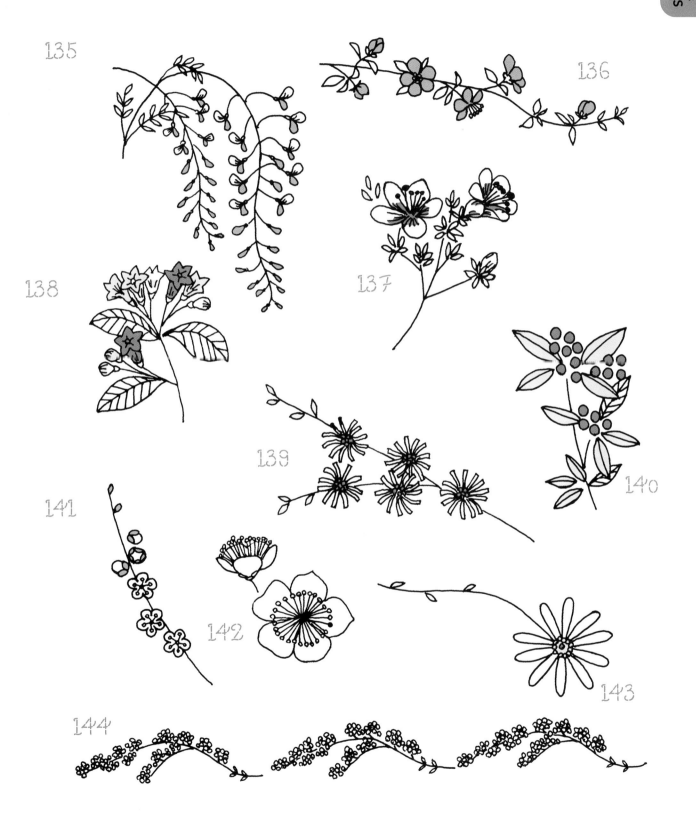

135

136

138

137

140

139

141

142

143

144

Flower Branches

Photos: Page 21

- ■ ○ = Number of strands (use 2 strands, unless otherwise noted)
- ■ # = Color number
- ■ Wrap all French knots once, unless otherwise noted.

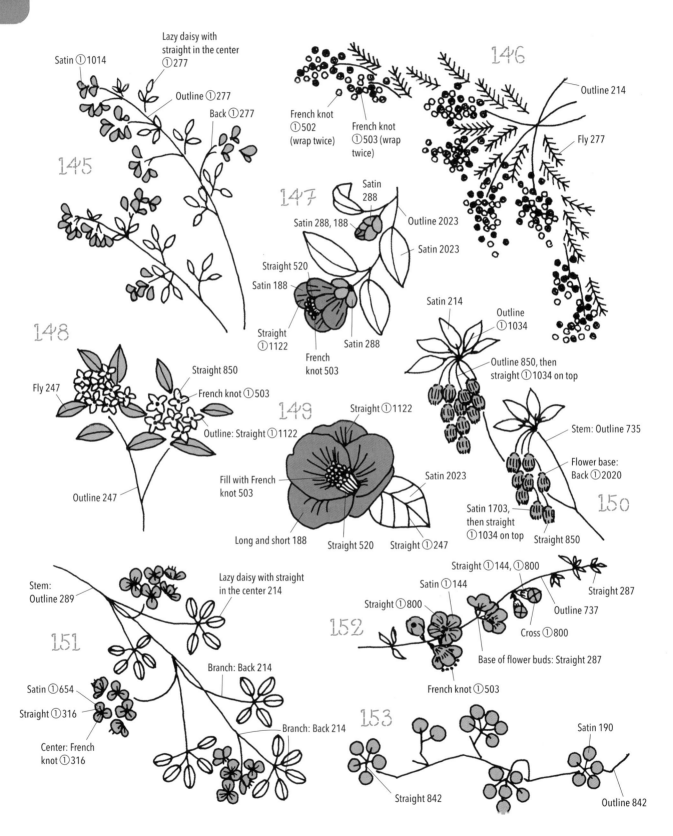

145

Satin ①1014

Lazy daisy with straight in the center ①277

Outline ①277

Back ①277

146

French knot ①502 (wrap twice)

French knot ①503 (wrap twice)

Outline 214

Fly 277

147

Satin 288

Satin 288, 188

Outline 2023

Satin 2023

Straight 520

Satin 188

Straight ①1122

French knot 503

Satin 288

Satin 214

Outline ①1034

Outline 850, then straight ①1034 on top

148

Fly 247

Straight 850

French knot ①503

Outline: Straight ①1122

Outline 247

149

Straight ①1122

Fill with French knot 503

Long and short 188

Satin 2023

Straight 520

Straight ①247

Stem: Outline 735

Flower base: Back ①2020

150

Satin 1703, then straight ①1034 on top

Straight 850

151

Stem: Outline 289

Lazy daisy with straight in the center 214

Branch: Back 214

Satin ①654

Straight ①316

Center: French knot ①316

Branch: Back 214

152

Straight ①144, ①800

Satin ①144

Straight ①800

Straight 287

Outline 737

Cross ①800

Base of flower buds: Straight 287

French knot ①503

153

Satin 190

Straight 842

Outline 842

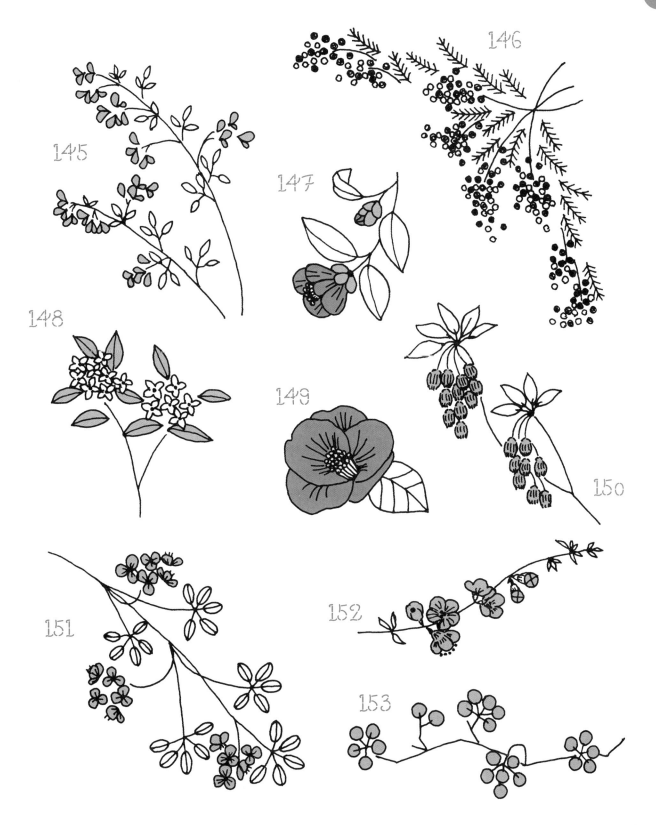

145
146
147
148
149
150
151
152
153

Fruit Trees

Photos: Page 22

■ ○ = Number of strands (use 1 strand, unless otherwise noted) ■ # = Color number ■ Use satin stitch, unless otherwise noted. ■ Wrap French knots twice, unless otherwise noted. ■ Use long and short ②520 for the bird bodies, French knot ①900 (wrap twice) for the bird eyes, and straight ①582 for the bird beaks.

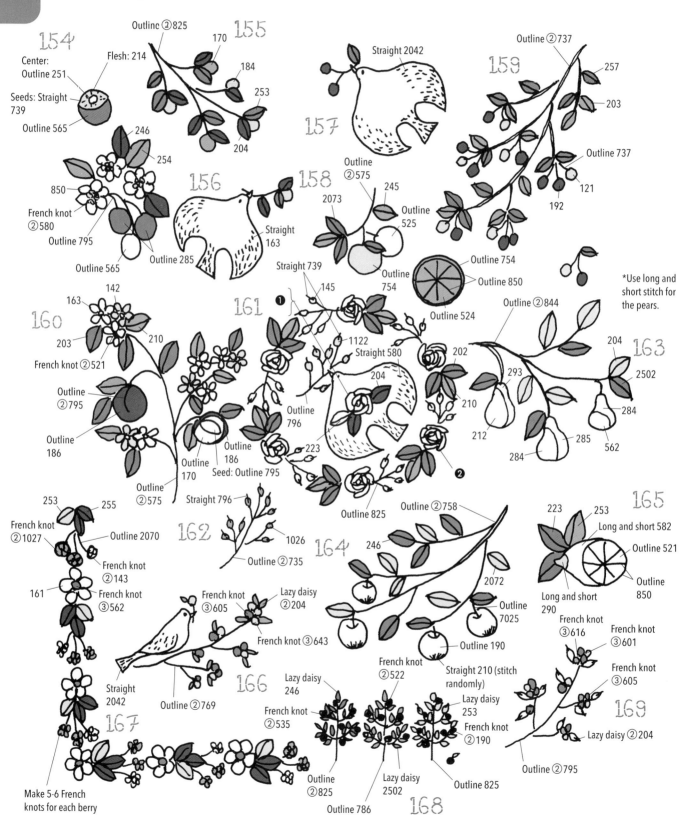

154

Center: Outline 251

Seeds: Straight 739

Outline 565

Flesh: 214

Outline ②825

155

170

184

253

204

246

254

850

French knot ②580

Outline 795

Outline 565

156

Straight 163

Outline 285

157

Straight 2042

158

Outline ②575

2073

245

Outline 525

Straight 739

145

Outline 754

Outline 754

Outline 850

Outline 524

159

Outline ②737

257

203

Outline 737

121

192

Outline ②844

*Use long and short stitch for the pears.

160

142

163

203

210

French knot ②521

Outline ②795

Outline 186

161

❶

1122

Straight 580

204

Outline 796

223

Outline 170

Outline 186

Seed: Outline 795

Outline ②575

Straight 796

202

210

204

212

284

293

285

562

284

163

2502

284

❷

Outline 825

Outline ②758

246

164

246

2072

Outline 7025

Outline 190

French knot ②522

Straight 210 (stitch randomly)

Lazy daisy 246

French knot ②535

Outline ②825

Lazy daisy 2502

Outline 825

Outline 786

168

165

223

253

Long and short 582

Outline 521

Outline 850

Long and short 290

French knot ③616

French knot ③601

French knot ③605

169

Lazy daisy ②204

Outline ②795

253

255

French knot ②1027

Outline 2070

French knot ②143

161

French knot ③562

162

1026

Outline ②735

French knot ③605

Lazy daisy ②204

French knot ③643

Straight 2042

Outline ②769

166

167

Make 5-6 French knots for each berry

Lazy daisy 253

French knot ②190

❶ Inner petals: Bullion ③163 (wrap 3 times)
Middle petals: Bullion ③1703 (wrap 6 times)
Outer petals: Bullion ③1705 (wrap 9 times)

❷ Inner petals: Bullion ③1705 (wrap 3 times)
Middle petals: Bullion ③1703 (wrap 6 times)
Outer petals: Bullion ③163 (wrap 9 times)

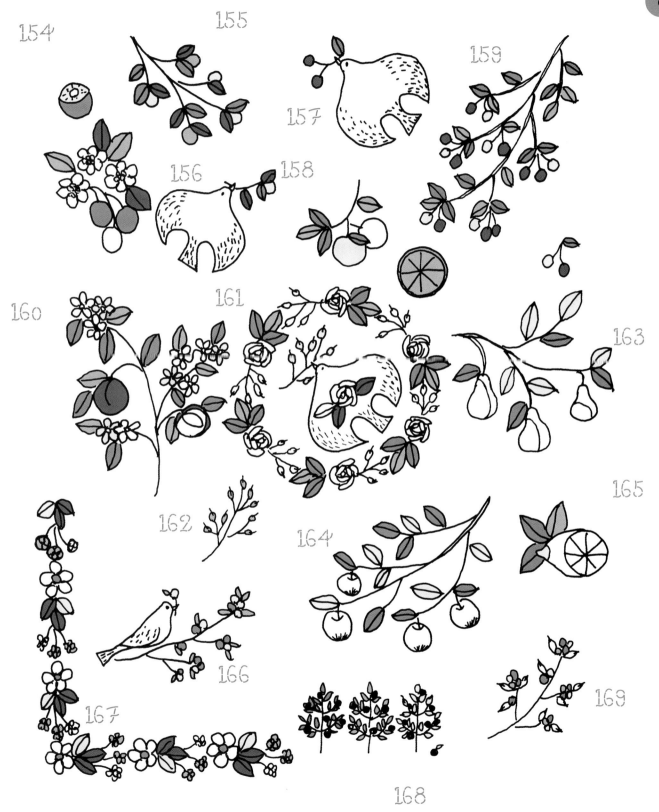

154

155

157

159

156

158

160

161

163

162

164

165

166

167

168

169

Fruit Trees

Photos: Page 23

■ ◯ = Number of strands (use 1 strand, unless otherwise noted)
■ # = Color number
■ Use satin stitch, unless otherwise noted.
■ Wrap French knots twice, unless otherwise noted.

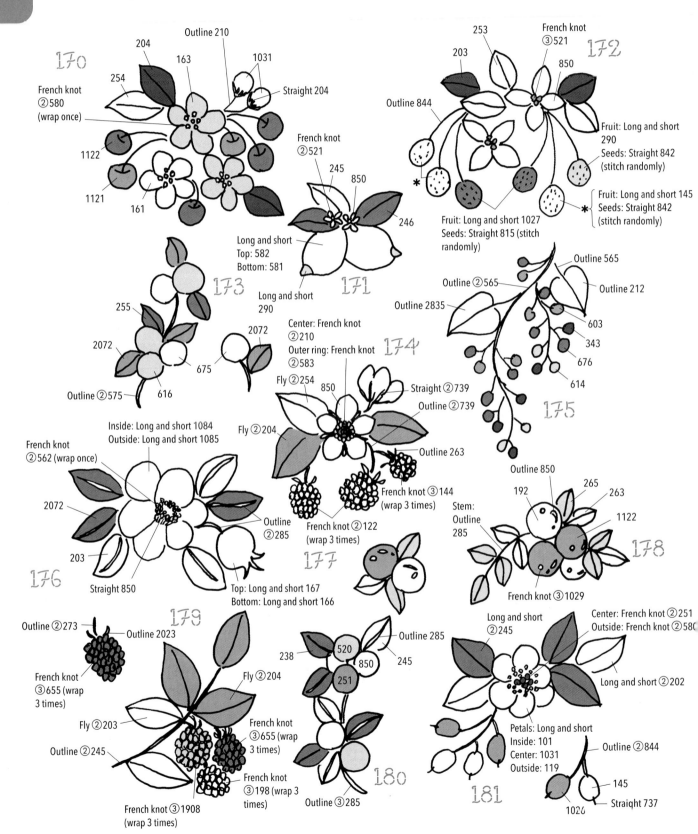

170
Outline 210
204
163
1031
254
Straight 204
French knot ②580 (wrap once)
1122
1121
161

171
French knot ②521
245
850
246
Long and short Top: 582 Bottom: 581
Long and short 290

172
253
French knot ③521
203
850
Outline 844
Fruit: Long and short 290
Seeds: Straight 842 (stitch randomly)
Fruit: Long and short 145
Seeds: Straight 842 (stitch randomly)
* Fruit: Long and short 1027
Seeds: Straight 815 (stitch randomly)

173
255
2072
675
Outline ②575
616
2072

174
Center: French knot ②210
Outer ring: French knot ②583
Fly ②254
850
Straight ②739
Fly ②204
Outline ②739
Outline 263
French knot ③144 (wrap 3 times)
French knot ②122 (wrap 3 times)
Outline ②285
Top: Long and short 167
Bottom: Long and short 166

175
Outline 565
Outline ②565
Outline 212
Outline 2835
603
343
676
614

176
Inside: Long and short 1084
Outside: Long and short 1085
French knot ②562 (wrap once)
2072
203
Straight 850

177
Outline 850
192
265
263
1122
Stem: Outline 285
French knot ③1029

178
Long and short ②245
Center: French knot ②251
Outside: French knot ②580
Long and short ②202
Petals: Long and short
Inside: 101
Center: 1031
Outside: 119

179
Outline ②273
Outline 2023
French knot ③655 (wrap 3 times)
Fly ②204
Fly ②203
Outline ②245
French knot ③655 (wrap 3 times)
French knot ③198 (wrap 3 times)
French knot ③1908 (wrap 3 times)

180
238
520
850
251
Outline 285
245
Outline ③285

181
Outline ②844
145
Straight 737
1026

170

172

173

171

174

175

176

177

178

179

180

181

Herbs

Photos: Page 24

■ ◯ = Number of strands (use 2 strands, unless otherwise noted)
■ # = Color number

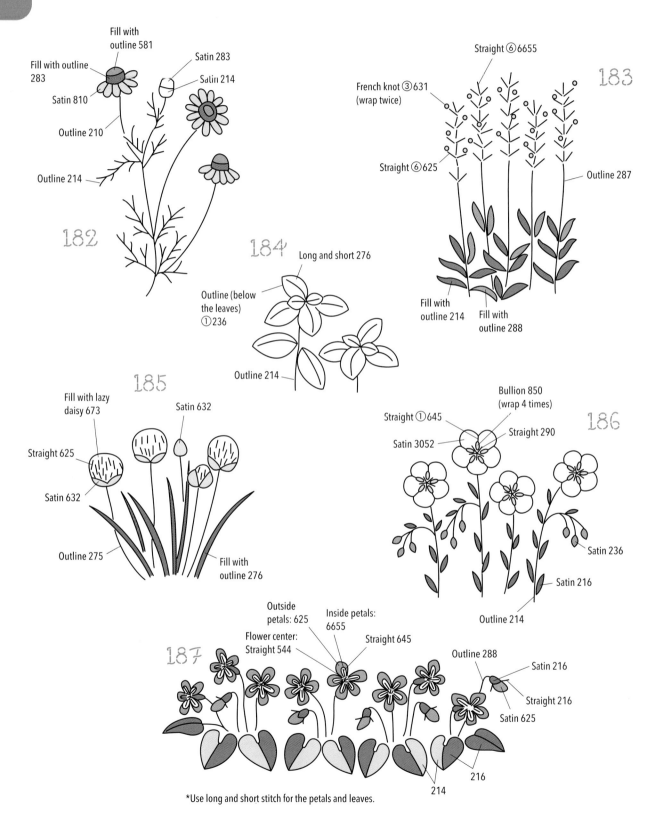

182

Fill with outline 581

Fill with outline 283

Satin 810

Satin 283

Satin 214

Outline 210

Outline 214

183

Straight ⑥6655

French knot ③631 (wrap twice)

Straight ⑥625

Outline 287

Fill with outline 214

Fill with outline 288

184

Long and short 276

Outline (below the leaves) ①236

Outline 214

185

Fill with lazy daisy 673

Satin 632

Straight 625

Satin 632

Outline 275

Fill with outline 276

186

Bullion 850 (wrap 4 times)

Straight ①645

Straight 290

Satin 3052

Satin 236

Satin 216

Outline 214

187

Outside petals: 625

Inside petals: 6655

Flower center: Straight 544

Straight 645

Outline 288

Satin 216

Straight 216

Satin 625

216

214

*Use long and short stitch for the petals and leaves.

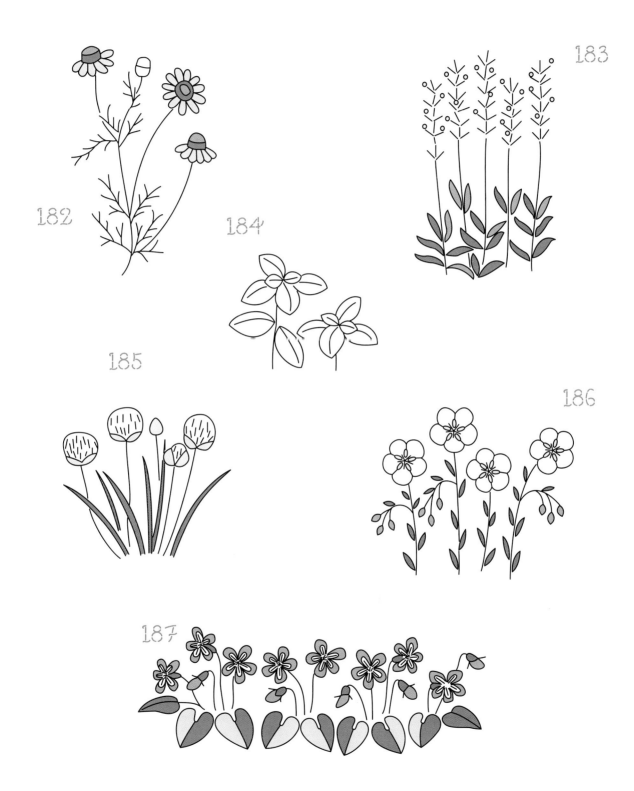

182

183

184

185

186

187

Herbs

Photos: Page 25

■ ◯ = Number of strands (use 2 strands, unless otherwise noted)
■ # = Color number

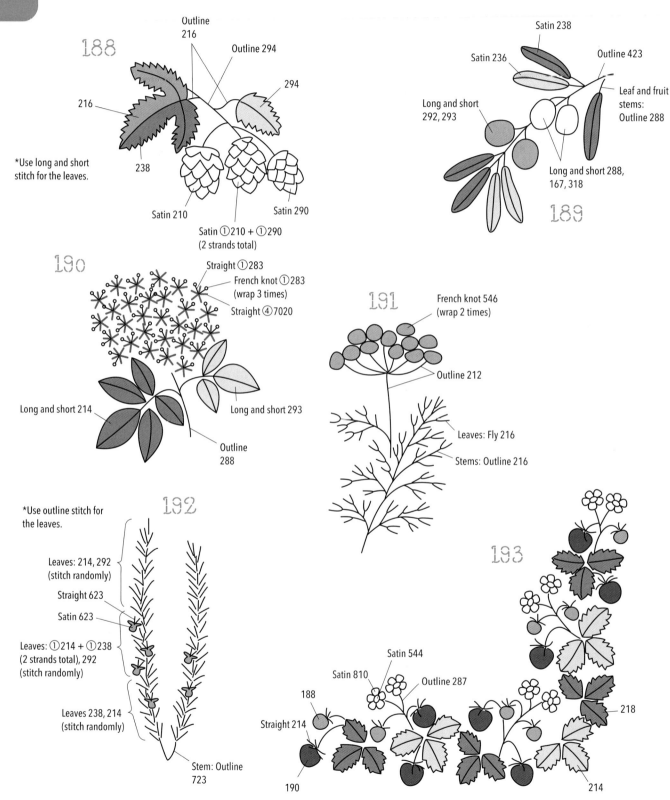

188

Outline 216
Outline 294
294
216
238
*Use long and short stitch for the leaves.
Satin 210
Satin ①210 + ①290 (2 strands total)
Satin 290

189

Satin 238
Satin 236
Outline 423
Leaf and fruit stems: Outline 288
Long and short 292, 293
Long and short 288, 167, 318

190

Straight ①283
French knot ①283 (wrap 3 times)
Straight ④7020
Long and short 214
Long and short 293
Outline 288

191

French knot 546 (wrap 2 times)
Outline 212
Leaves: Fly 216
Stems: Outline 216

192

*Use outline stitch for the leaves.
Leaves: 214, 292 (stitch randomly)
Straight 623
Satin 623
Leaves: ①214 + ①238 (2 strands total), 292 (stitch randomly)
Leaves 238, 214 (stitch randomly)
Stem: Outline 723

193

Satin 544
Satin 810
Outline 287
188
Straight 214
190
218
214

*Use long and short stitch for the fruit and the leaves.

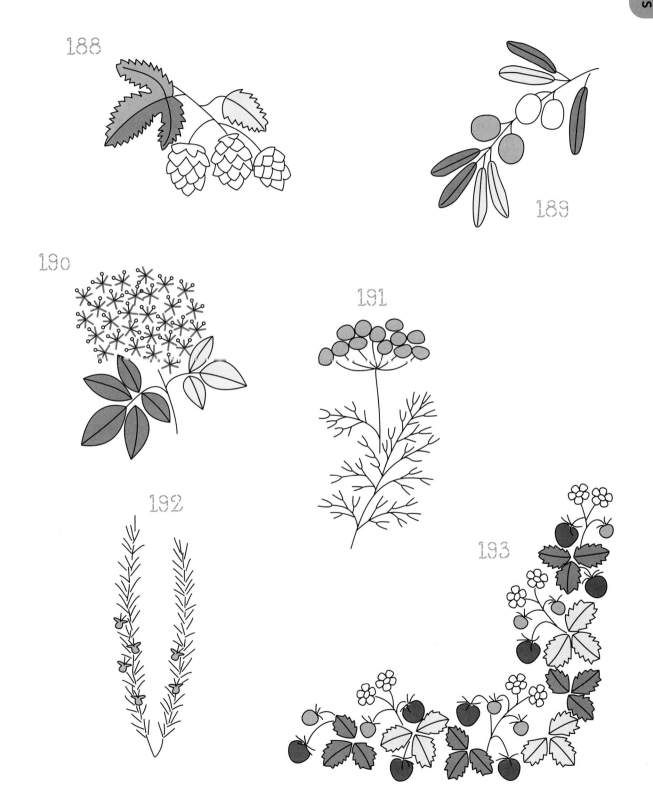

188

189

190

191

192

193

Wildflowers & Mushrooms

Photos: Page 26

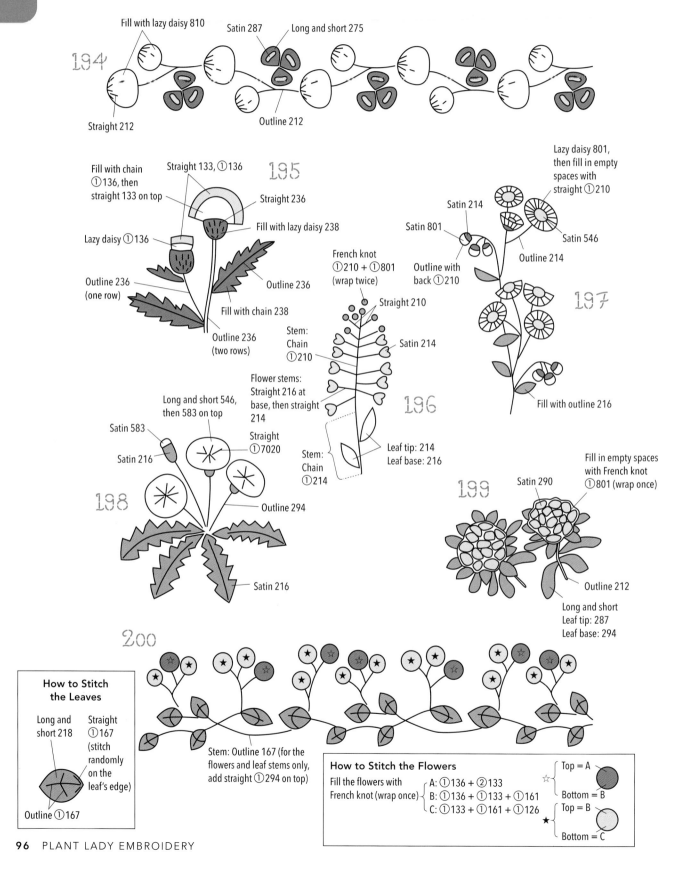

194

Fill with lazy daisy 810

Satin 287

Long and short 275

Straight 212

Outline 212

195

Fill with chain ①136, then straight 133 on top

Straight 133, ①136

Straight 236

Fill with lazy daisy 238

Lazy daisy ①136

Outline 236 (one row)

Outline 236

Fill with chain 238

Outline 236 (two rows)

196

French knot ①210 + ①801 (wrap twice)

Straight 210

Stem: Chain ①210

Satin 214

Flower stems: Straight 216 at base, then straight 214

Stem: Chain ①214

Leaf tip: 214
Leaf base: 216

197

Lazy daisy 801, then fill in empty spaces with straight ①210

Satin 214

Satin 801

Outline 214

Satin 546

Outline with back ①210

Fill with outline 216

198

Long and short 546, then 583 on top

Satin 583

Straight ①7020

Satin 216

Outline 294

Satin 216

199

Fill in empty spaces with French knot ①801 (wrap once)

Satin 290

Outline 212

Long and short
Leaf tip: 287
Leaf base: 294

200

How to Stitch the Leaves

Long and short 218

Straight ①167 (stitch randomly on the leaf's edge)

Outline ①167

Stem: Outline 167 (for the flowers and leaf stems only, add straight ①294 on top)

How to Stitch the Flowers

Fill the flowers with French knot (wrap once)

A: ①136 + ②133
B: ①136 + ①133 + ①161
C: ①133 + ①161 + ①126

☆ Top = A
Bottom = B

★ Top = B
Bottom = C

■ ○ = Number of strands (use 2 strands, unless otherwise noted)
■ # = Color number

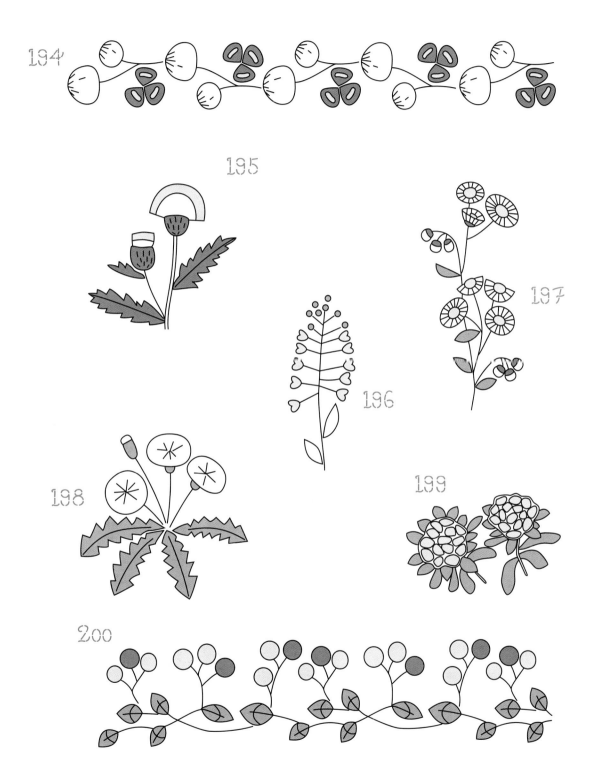

194

195

196

197

198

199

200

Wildflowers & Mushrooms

Photos: Page 27

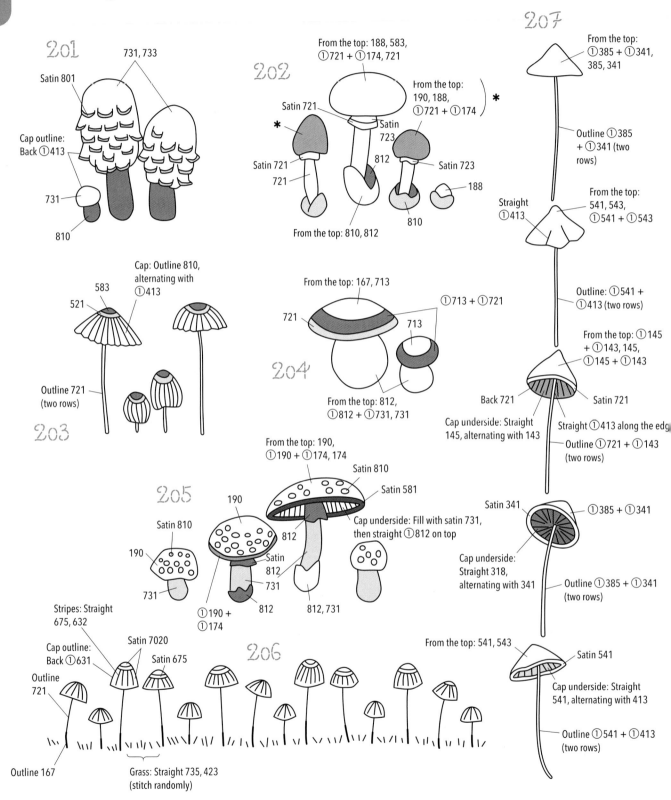

201

731, 733

Satin 801

Cap outline:
Back ①413

731

810

202

From the top: 188, 583,
①721 + ①174, 721

From the top:
190, 188,
①721 + ①174 ⟩ *

Satin 721

* Satin
723

Satin 721

721

812

Satin 723

188

810

From the top: 810, 812

207

From the top:
①385 + ①341,
385, 341

Outline ①385
+ ①341 (two
rows)

From the top:
541, 543,
①541 + ①543

Straight
①413

Outline: ①541 +
①413 (two rows)

From the top: ①145
+ ①143, 145,
①145 + ①143

Back 721

Satin 721

Cap underside: Straight
145, alternating with 143

Straight ①413 along the edge

Outline ①721 + ①143
(two rows)

Satin 341

①385 + ①341

Cap underside:
Straight 318,
alternating with 341

Outline ①385 + ①341
(two rows)

Cap: Outline 810,
alternating with
①413

583

521

Outline 721
(two rows)

203

From the top: 167, 713

721

①713 + ①721

713

204

From the top: 812,
①812 + ①731, 731

205

Satin 810

190

190

731

From the top: 190,
①190 + ①174, 174

Satin 810

Satin 581

Cap underside: Fill with satin 731,
then straight ①812 on top

812

Satin
812

731

①190 +
①174

812

812, 731

From the top: 541, 543

Satin 541

Cap underside: Straight
541, alternating with 413

Outline ①541 + ①413
(two rows)

206

Stripes: Straight
675, 632

Cap outline:
Back ①631

Satin 7020

Satin 675

Outline
721

Outline 167

Grass: Straight 735, 423
(stitch randomly)

- ○ = Number of strands (use 2 strands, unless otherwise noted)
- # = Color number
- Use long and short stitch, unless otherwise noted.
- When there are multiple color numbers listed, stitch in a gradation for shading.

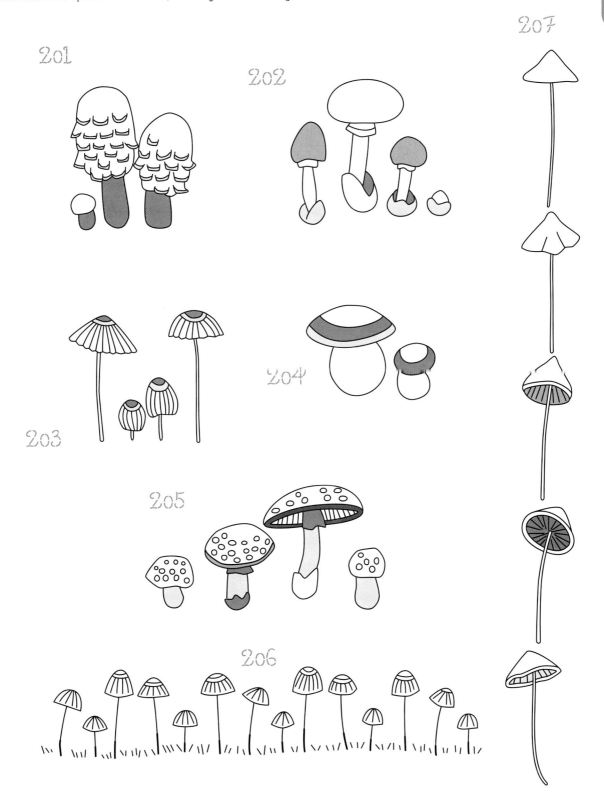

201

202

203

204

205

206

207

Cacti & Succulents

Photos: Page 28

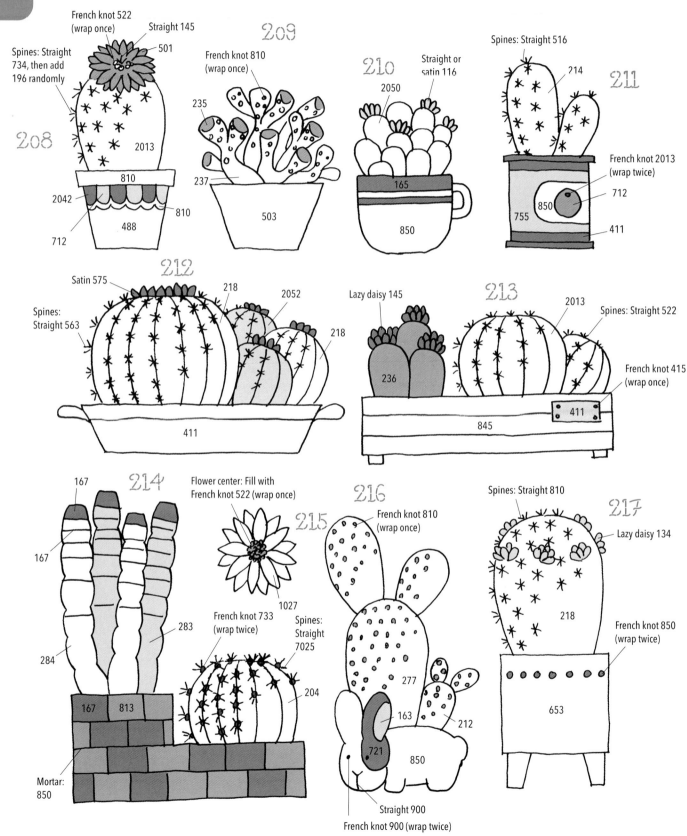

208

French knot 522 (wrap once)

Straight 145

501

Spines: Straight 734, then add 196 randomly

2013

810

2042

712

488

810

209

French knot 810 (wrap once)

235

237

503

210

Straight or satin 116

2050

165

850

211

Spines: Straight 516

214

French knot 2013 (wrap twice)

712

850

755

411

212

Satin 575

Spines: Straight 563

218

2052

218

411

213

Lazy daisy 145

2013

Spines: Straight 522

French knot 415 (wrap once)

236

411

845

214

167

167

283

284

167

813

Mortar: 850

Flower center: Fill with French knot 522 (wrap once)

215

1027

French knot 733 (wrap twice)

Spines: Straight 7025

204

216

French knot 810 (wrap once)

277

163

212

721

850

Straight 900

French knot 900 (wrap twice)

217

Spines: Straight 810

Lazy daisy 134

218

French knot 850 (wrap twice)

653

■ ◯ = Number of strands (use 2 strands, unless otherwise noted) ■ # = Color number
■ Thick outlines are chain ②900 and thin outlines are back ②900. ■ Fill all motifs with chain ③,
unless otherwise noted. Fill any gaps between the chain stitches using satin or straight stitch.

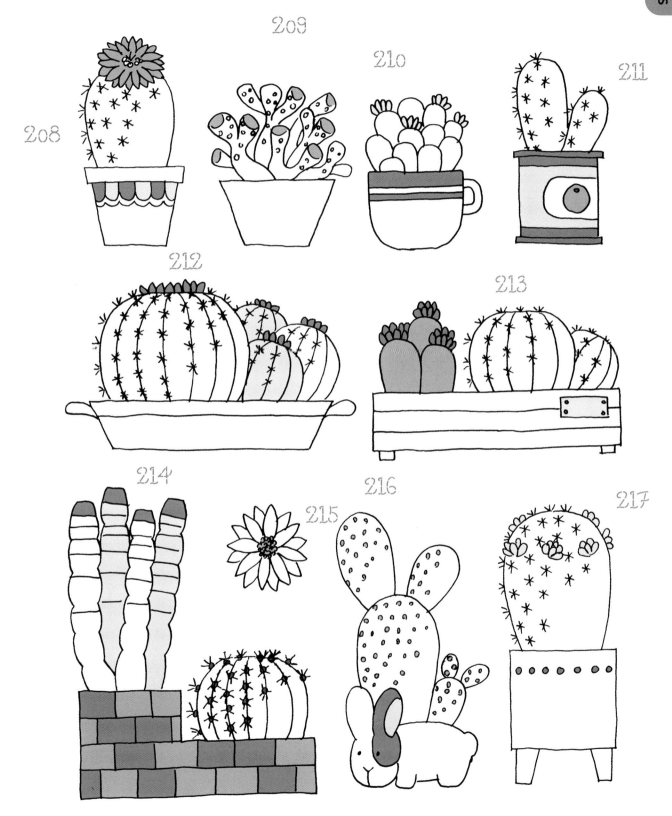

Cacti & Succulents

Photos: Page 29

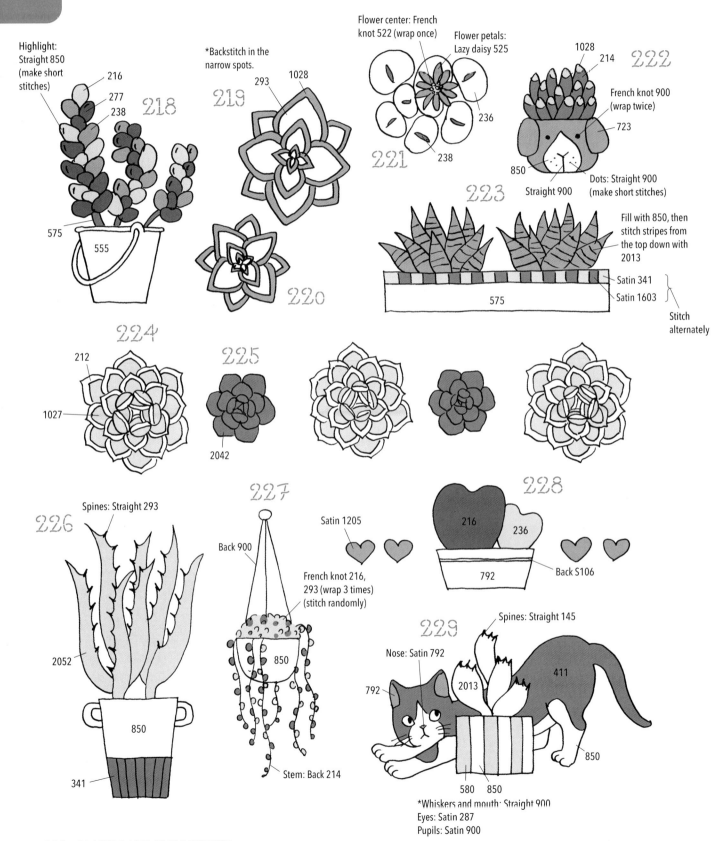

218
Highlight: Straight 850 (make short stitches)
216
277
238
575
555

219
*Backstitch in the narrow spots.
293
1028
220

221
Flower center: French knot 522 (wrap once)
Flower petals: Lazy daisy 525
236
238

222
1028
214
French knot 900 (wrap twice)
723
850
Straight 900
Dots: Straight 900 (make short stitches)

223
Fill with 850, then stitch stripes from the top down with 2013
Satin 341
Satin 1603
Stitch alternately
575

224
212
1027

225
2042

226
Spines: Straight 293
2052
850
341

227
Satin 1205
Back 900
French knot 216, 293 (wrap 3 times) (stitch randomly)
850
Stem: Back 214

228
216
236
792
Back S106

229
Spines: Straight 145
Nose: Satin 792
792
2013
411
580 850
850
*Whiskers and mouth: Straight 900
Eyes: Satin 287
Pupils: Satin 900

■ ◯ = Number of strands (use 2 strands, unless otherwise noted) ■ # = Color number
■ Thick outlines are chain ②900 and thin outlines are back ②900. ■ Fill all motifs with chain ③,
unless otherwise noted. Fill any gaps between the chain stitches using satin or straight stitch.

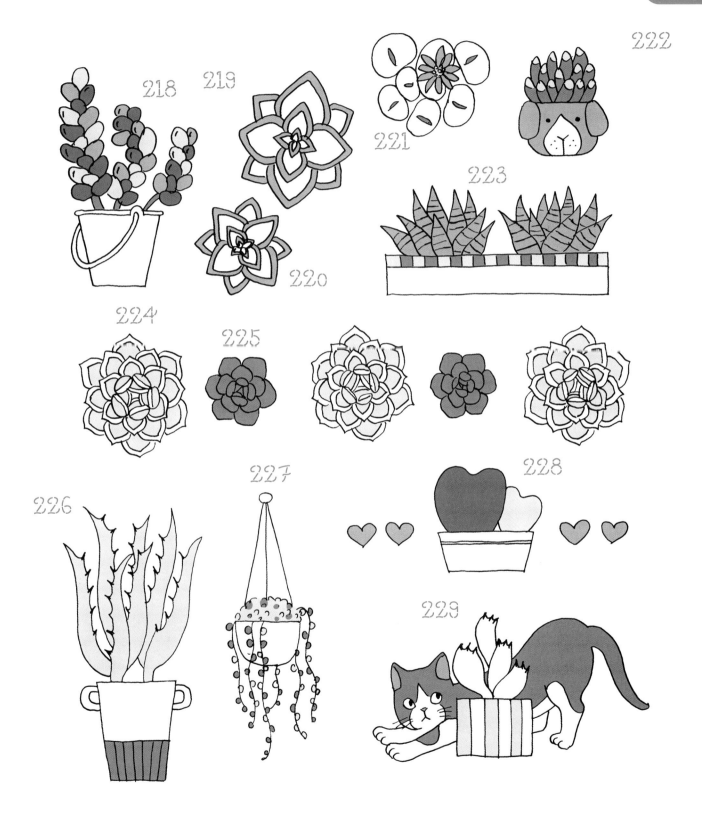

Tropical Plants

Photos: Page 30

- ■ ○ = Number of strands (use 2 strands, unless otherwise noted)
- ■ # = Color number
- ■ Use backstitch, unless otherwise noted.

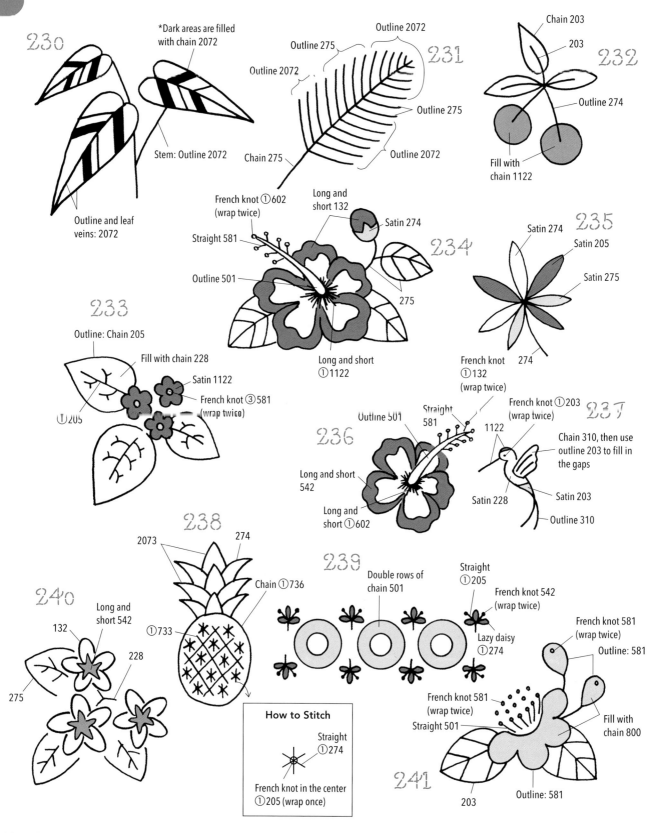

230
*Dark areas are filled with chain 2072
Stem: Outline 2072
Outline and leaf veins: 2072

231
Outline 2072
Outline 275
Outline 2072
Outline 2072
Outline 275
Outline 2072
Chain 275

232
Chain 203
203
Outline 274
Fill with chain 1122

233
Outline: Chain 205
Fill with chain 228
Satin 1122
French knot ③581 (wrap twice)
①205

234
French knot ①602 (wrap twice)
Long and short 132
Satin 274
Straight 581
Outline 501
275
Long and short ①1122

235
Satin 274
Satin 205
Satin 275
French knot ①132 (wrap twice)
274

236
Outline 501
Straight 581
Long and short 542
Long and short ①602

237
French knot ①203 (wrap twice)
1122
Chain 310, then use outline 203 to fill in the gaps
Satin 228
Satin 203
Outline 310

238
2073
274
Chain ①736
①733

239
Double rows of chain 501
Straight ①205
French knot 542 (wrap twice)
Lazy daisy ①274

240
Long and short 542
132
228
275

241
French knot 581 (wrap twice)
Outline: 581
French knot 581 (wrap twice)
Straight 501
Fill with chain 800
Outline: 581
203

How to Stitch
Straight ①274
French knot in the center ①205 (wrap once)

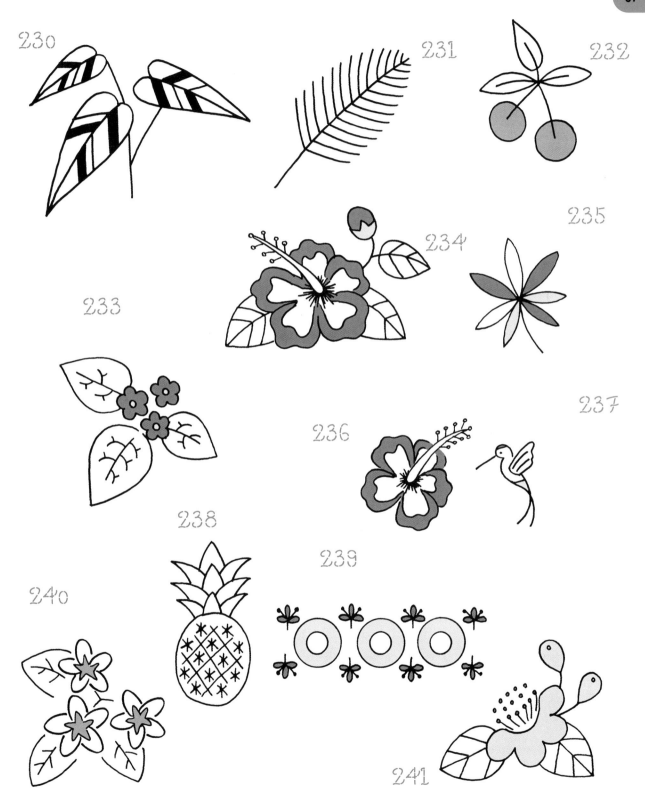

230

231

232

235

234

233

237

236

238

239

240

241

Tropical Plants

Photos: Page 31

- ■ ○ = Number of strands (use 2 strands, unless otherwise noted)
- ■ # = Color number
- ■ Use backstitch, unless otherwise noted.

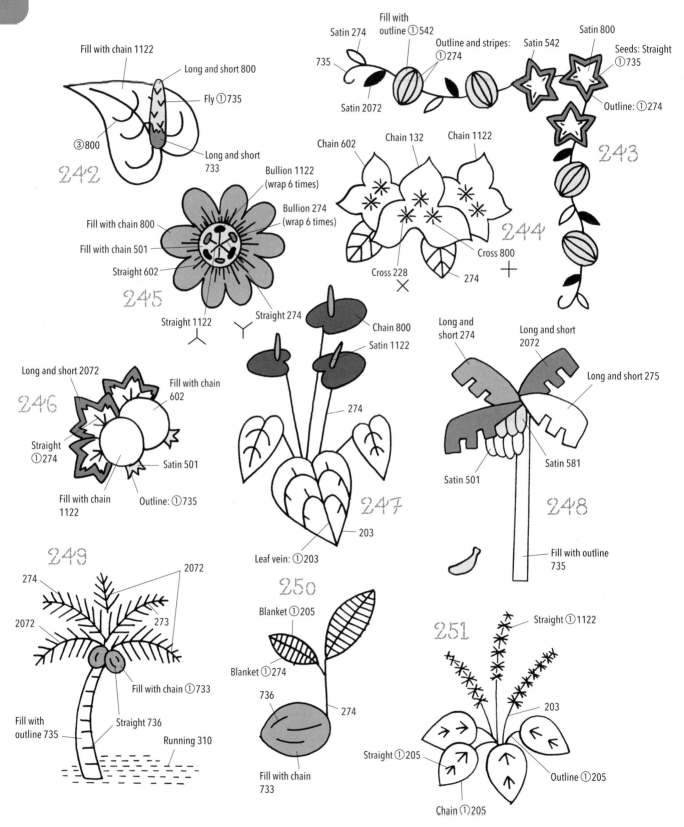

242
- Fill with chain 1122
- Long and short 800
- Fly ①735
- ③800
- Long and short 733

243
- Satin 274
- 735
- Satin 2072
- Fill with outline ①542
- Outline and stripes: ①274
- Satin 542
- Satin 800
- Seeds: Straight ①735
- Outline: ①274

244
- Chain 602
- Chain 132
- Chain 1122
- Cross 228
- Cross 800
- 274

245
- Bullion 1122 (wrap 6 times)
- Bullion 274 (wrap 6 times)
- Fill with chain 800
- Fill with chain 501
- Straight 602
- Straight 1122
- Straight 274

246
- Long and short 2072
- Fill with chain 602
- Straight ①274
- Satin 501
- Fill with chain 1122
- Outline: ①735

247
- Chain 800
- Satin 1122
- 274
- 203
- Leaf vein: ①203

248
- Long and short 274
- Long and short 2072
- Long and short 275
- Satin 581
- Satin 501
- Fill with outline 735

249
- 2072
- 274
- 2072
- 273
- Fill with chain ①733
- Fill with outline 735
- Straight 736
- Running 310

250
- Blanket ①205
- Blanket ①274
- 736
- 274
- Fill with chain 733

251
- Straight ①1122
- 203
- Straight ①205
- Chain ①205
- Outline ①205

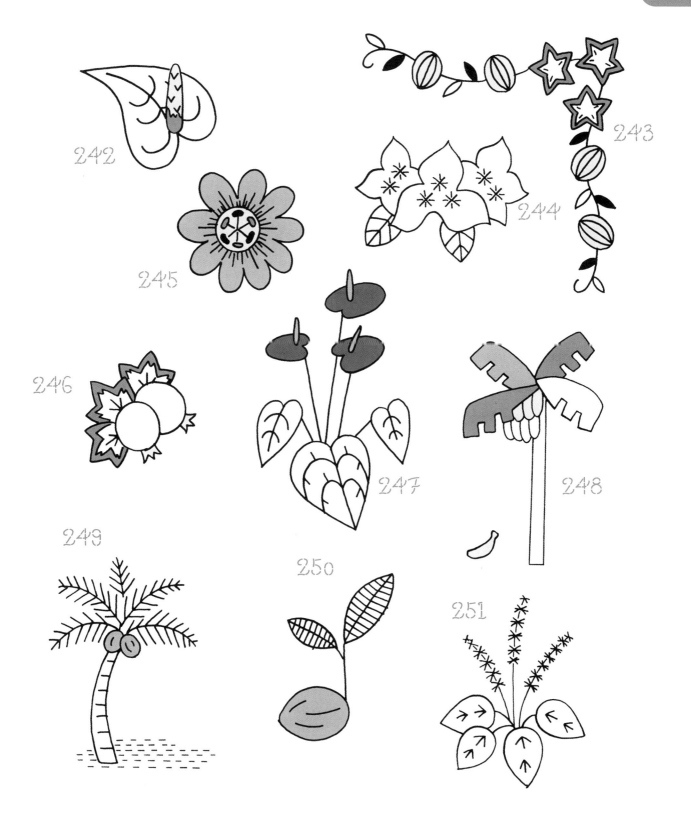

242

243

244

245

246

247

248

249

250

251

Foliage Plants

Photos: Page 32

- ■ ○ = Number of strands (use 2 strands, unless otherwise noted)
- ■ # = Color number
- ■ Use backstitch, unless otherwise noted.

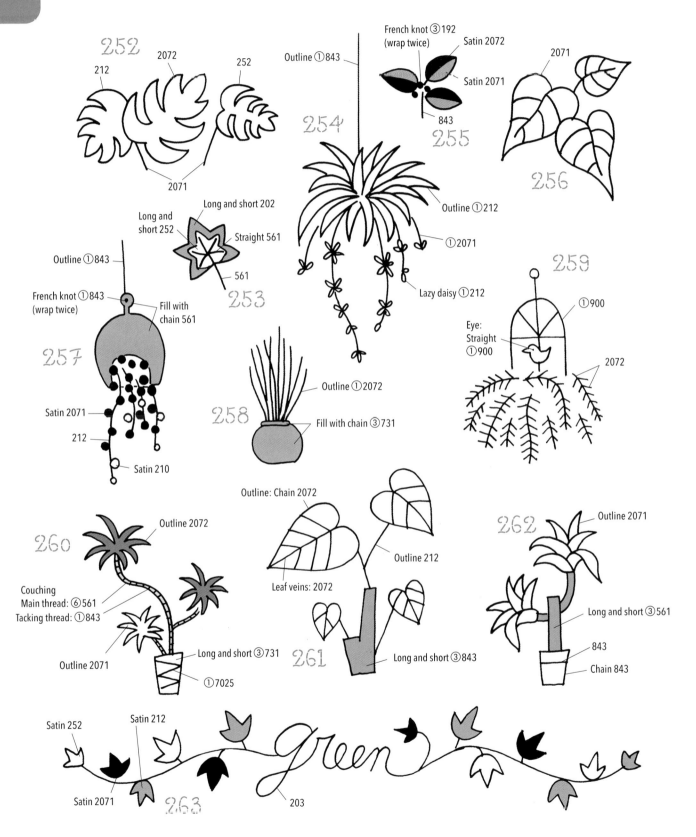

252
- 2072
- 212
- 252
- 2071

254
- Outline ①843
- French knot ③192 (wrap twice)
- Satin 2072
- Satin 2071
- 843

255

256
- 2071

- Outline ①212
- ①2071
- Lazy daisy ①212

253
- Long and short 252
- Long and short 202
- Straight 561
- 561

257
- Outline ①843
- French knot ①843 (wrap twice)
- Fill with chain 561
- Satin 2071
- 212
- Satin 210

258
- Outline ①2072
- Fill with chain ③731

259
- Eye: Straight ①900
- ①900
- 2072

260
- Outline 2072
- Couching
  Main thread: ⑥561
  Tacking thread: ①843
- Outline 2071
- Long and short ③731
- ①7025

261
- Outline: Chain 2072
- Outline 212
- Leaf veins: 2072
- Long and short ③843

262
- Outline 2071
- Long and short ③561
- 843
- Chain 843

263
- Satin 252
- Satin 212
- Satin 2071
- 203

green

252

254

255

256

253

259

257

258

260

261

262

263

green

Foliage Plants

Photos: Page 33

■ ○ = Number of strands (use 2 strands, unless otherwise noted)
■ # = Color number
■ Use backstitch, unless otherwise noted.

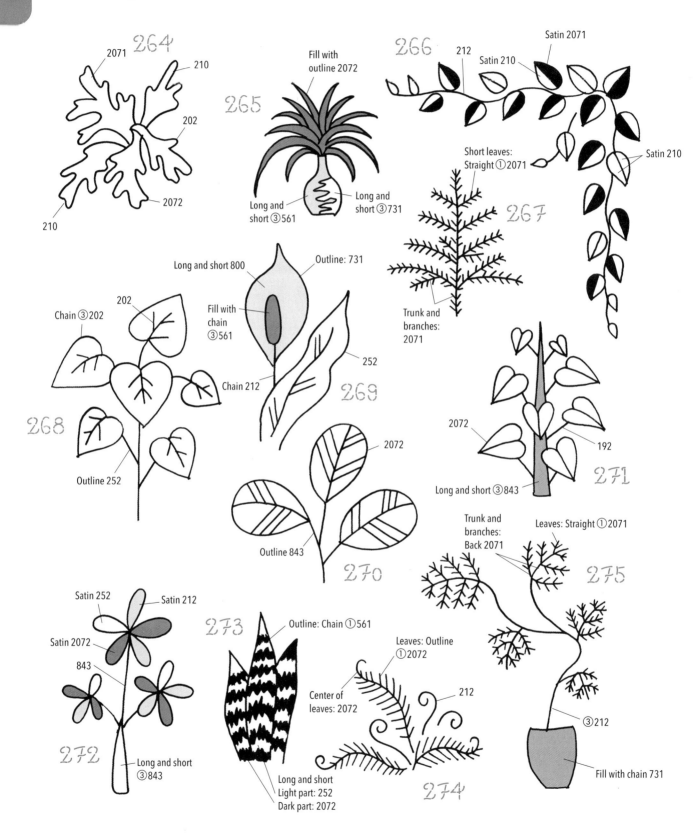

264 — 2071, 210, 202, 2072, 210

265 — Fill with outline 2072; Long and short ③561; Long and short ③731

266 — 212, Satin 210, Satin 2071, Satin 210, Satin 210

267 — Short leaves: Straight ①2071; Trunk and branches: 2071

268 — Chain ③202, 202, Outline 252

269 — Long and short 800, Outline: 731, Fill with chain ③561, Chain 212, 252

270 — 2072, Outline 843

271 — 2072, 192, Long and short ③843

272 — Satin 252, Satin 212, Satin 2072, 843, Long and short ③843

273 — Outline: Chain ①561; Long and short Light part: 252 Dark part: 2072

274 — Leaves: Outline ①2072; Center of leaves: 2072; 212

275 — Trunk and branches: Back 2071; Leaves: Straight ①2071; ③212; Fill with chain 731

110   PLANT LADY EMBROIDERY

264

266

265

267

268

269

270

271

272

273

274

275

Aquatic Plants

Photos: Page 34

- ■ ○ = Number of strands (use 3 strands, unless otherwise noted)
- ■ # = Color number
- ■ Use satin stitch, unless otherwise noted.
- ■ Wrap French knots twice, unless otherwise noted.

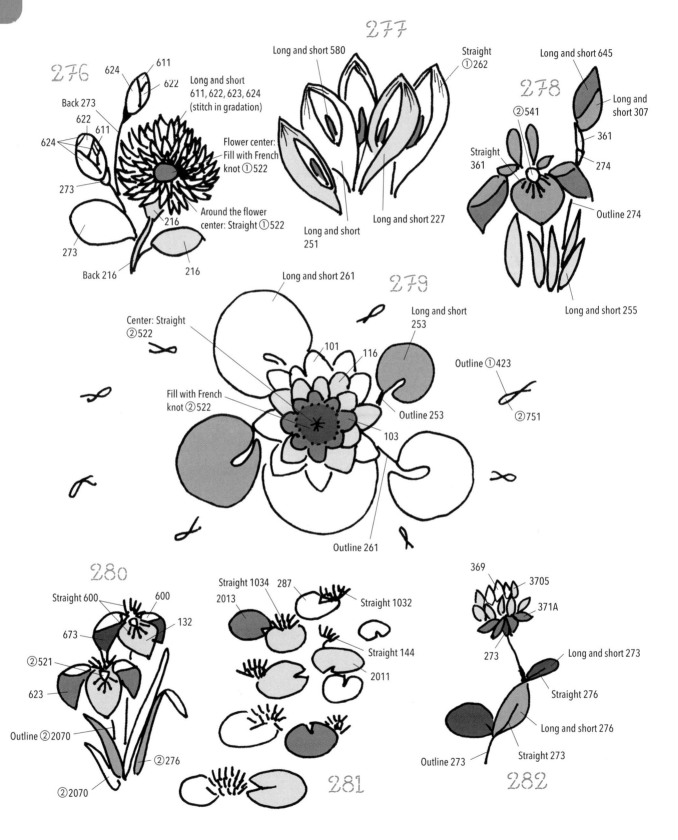

276

611
624
622

Long and short 611, 622, 623, 624 (stitch in gradation)

Back 273
622
611
624

273

Flower center: Fill with French knot ①522

Around the flower center: Straight ①522

216
273
Back 216
216

277

Long and short 580

Straight ①262

Long and short 227

Long and short 251

278

Long and short 645

②541

Long and short 307

361

274

Straight 361

Outline 274

Long and short 255

279

Long and short 261

Center: Straight ②522

Long and short 253

101
116

Fill with French knot ②522

Outline ①423

②751

Outline 253

103

Outline 261

280

Straight 600
600

673
132

②521

623

Outline ②2070

②276

②2070

281

Straight 1034
287
2013

Straight 1032

Straight 144

2011

282

369
3705

371A

273

Long and short 273

Straight 276

Long and short 276

Outline 273

Straight 273

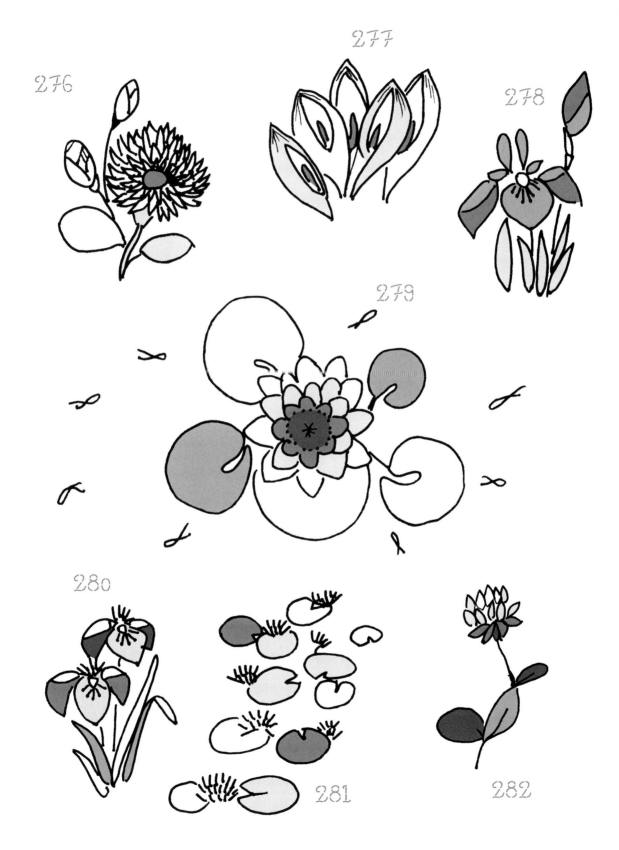

276

277

278

279

280

281

282

Aquatic Plants

Photos: Page 35

- ■ ○ = Number of strands (use 3 strands, unless otherwise noted)
- ■ # = Color number
- ■ Use satin stitch, unless otherwise noted.
- ■ Wrap French knots once, unless otherwise noted.
- ■ The two digit numbers represent variegated threads.

283

Fly 32

2042 Blanket 2042

Fly 38

Chain 2042

Fly 72

Blanket 2042

Water surface: Straight 11

Fly 252

French knot ②252
(wrap twice)

Fly 277

②753

264 Back 264

Fly 289

2065

Fill with
French knot
⑥22

Lettering: Back 354

②758 WaterGarden

②754

238

288

2051

Lilypads: 288, 2050, 2051, 238

2050

Fill randomly with French knot 288, 2050, 2051, 238

Water lily flower.
Straight ⑥36

Water Garden

English Garden

Photos: Page 36

- ■ ○ = Number of strands (use 3 strands, unless otherwise noted)
- ■ # = Color number
- ■ Wrap French knots once, unless otherwise noted.
- ■ The two digit numbers represent variegated threads.

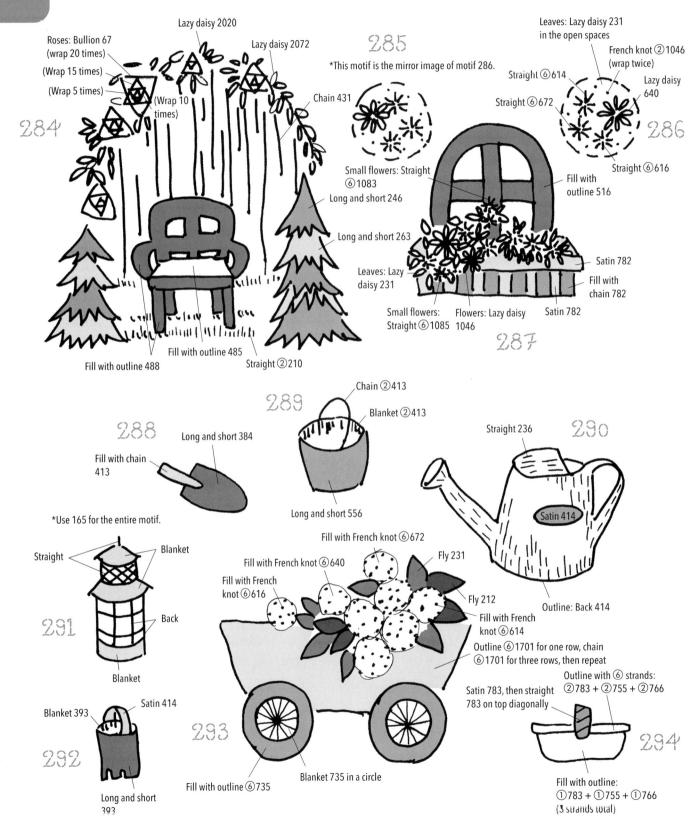

284

Roses: Bullion 67 (wrap 20 times)

(Wrap 15 times)

(Wrap 5 times)

(Wrap 10 times)

Lazy daisy 2020

Lazy daisy 2072

Chain 431

Fill with outline 488

Fill with outline 485

Straight ②210

285

*This motif is the mirror image of motif 286.

Small flowers: Straight ⑥1083

Long and short 246

Long and short 263

Leaves: Lazy daisy 231

Small flowers: Straight ⑥1085

Flowers: Lazy daisy 1046

286

Leaves: Lazy daisy 231 in the open spaces

French knot ②1046 (wrap twice)

Lazy daisy 640

Straight ⑥614

Straight ⑥672

Straight ⑥616

Fill with outline 516

Satin 782

Fill with chain 782

Satin 782

287

288

Fill with chain 413

Long and short 384

*Use 165 for the entire motif.

Straight

Blanket

Back

Blanket

291

Blanket 393

Satin 414

292

Long and short 393

289

Chain ②413

Blanket ②413

Long and short 556

293

Fill with French knot ⑥672

Fill with French knot ⑥640

Fill with French knot ⑥616

Fly 231

Fly 212

Fill with French knot ⑥614

Outline ⑥1701 for one row, chain ⑥1701 for three rows, then repeat

Fill with outline ⑥735

Blanket 735 in a circle

290

Straight 236

Satin 414

Outline: Back 414

294

Satin 783, then straight 783 on top diagonally

Outline with ⑥ strands: ②783 + ②755 + ②766

Fill with outline: ①783 + ①755 + ①766 (3 strands total)

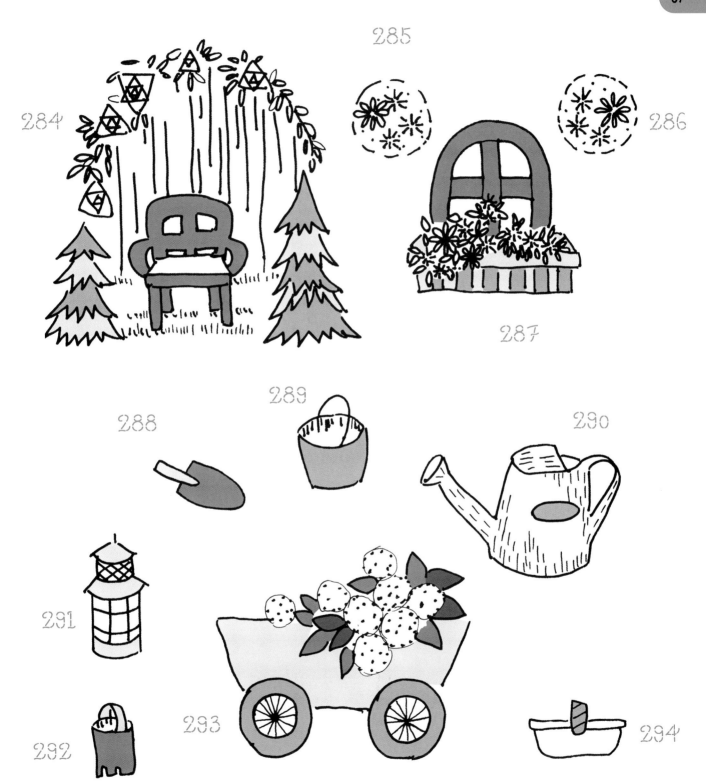

285

284

286

287

288

289

290

291

292

293

294

English Garden

Photos: Page 37

■ ○ = Number of strands (use 2 strands, unless otherwise noted) ■ # = Color number
■ Wrap all French knots twice, unless otherwise noted. ■ The two digit numbers
represent variegated threads. ■ The multicolor roofs in motifs 295 and 300 are stitched
with a multicolor thread that has 8 different colors in one skein.

295

Straight ⑥3042 vertically, then
horizontally, then cross 3043
at the intersections

Outline: Couching
Main thread: ⑥3042
Tacking thread: 3043

Satin 0003

Satin
580

Back 3043

Back 3043

296

*Roses are all bullion
③62 with the center
wrapped 5 times. For
each round, increase
number of wraps by 5.

Stem: Outline 293   Stem: Outline 275

Leaves: Fly 293   Leaves: Fly 275

(Wrap
15 times)
(Wrap
10 times)
(Wrap
5 times)

Couching ③765

Leaves: Lazy daisy
③228

Flower petals:
Satin or straight 184

Flower: Satin 38

Flower centers:
French knot 184

Stem:
Outline 2445

Leaves: Satin 205

Blanket ③815

Buds: Bullion
③62 (wrap
7 times)

Straight 815
(stitch multiple
times)

297

French knot
3052

298

Satin 451   Satin 452   Satin 844

Straight 501

Straight 654

Leaves: Fly 254

Leaves: Fly 257

Straight 1121

Straight 1082
Blanket 503

Straight 621   Straight 531

Back 412

*For the flowers, work the
blanket stitch in a circle.

Blanket 502

Blanket 501

Fill with French
knot ③133

Stem: Outline +
French knot 2022

Blanket 102

Blanket 104

Leaves:
Satin
2022

Blanket 8803 in
a scale pattern

300

Fill with French knot ③135

Bullion 353, 354 (wrap
7 times), then fill the empty
spaces with straight 68

Leaves: Fill the empty
spaces with lazy daisy ③229

Chain ③342

Lazy daisy 17   Straight
792

French knot
196

Leaves: Straight ⑥68

Fill with
French knot
⑥68
(wrap once)

Chain 411

Fill with French knot
⑥36 (wrap once)

Fishbone 244

299

Blanket ③342
in a circle

Lazy daisy ①343   Lazy daisy
③229

Fill with
outline
③342

Fill with French
knot ⑥68
(wrap once)

Fly 61

Fishbone 203

Fishbone 204

295

296

297

298

300

299

ALSO AVAILABLE

Cat Lady Embroidery
978-1-58923-964-7

I Love My Dog Embroidery
978-1-63159-613-1

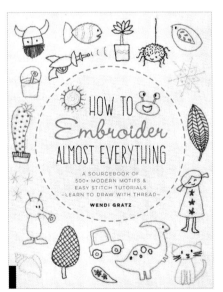

How to Embroider Almost Everything
978-1-63159-789-3

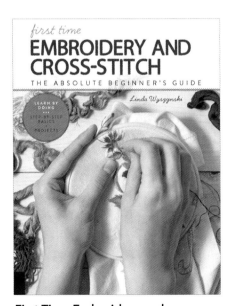

First Time Embroidery and Cross-Stitch
978-1-63159-797-8

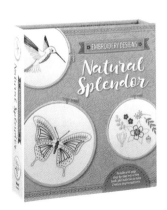

Embroidery Designs: Natural Splendor
978-0-76036-210-5